ISBN 978-1-333-51766-3
PIBN 10514476

This book is a reproduction of an important historical work. Forgotten Books uses
state-of-the-art technology to digitally reconstruct the work, preserving the original format
whilst repairing imperfections present in the aged copy. In rare cases, an imperfection in
the original, such as a blemish or missing page, may be replicated in our edition. We do,
however, repair the vast majority of imperfections successfully; any imperfections that
remain are intentionally left to preserve the state of such historical works.

English
Français
Deutsche
Italiano
Español
Português

www.forgottenbooks.com

Mythology Photography **Fiction**
Fishing Christianity **Art** Cooking
Essays Buddhism Freemasonry
Medicine **Biology** Music **Ancient
Egypt** Evolution Carpentry Physics
Dance Geology **Mathematics** Fitness
Shakespeare **Folklore** Yoga Marketing
Confidence Immortality Biographies
Poetry **Psychology** Witchcraft
Electronics Chemistry History **Law**
Accounting **Philosophy** Anthropology
Alchemy Drama Quantum Mechanics
Atheism Sexual Health **Ancient History**
Entrepreneurship Languages Sport
Paleontology Needlework Islam
Metaphysics Investment Archaeology
Parenting Statistics Criminology
Motivational

FOREST RUNES.

BY

GEORGE W. SEARS,

(NESSMUK).

NEW YORK:

FOREST AND STREAM PUBLISHING CO.,

1887.

DEDICATION.

TO MY BROTHER CHARLES.

NOT that the gift of poesy is mine,
    Nor that I claim the poet's meed of praise,
  But in remembrance of the golden days
  . Of youth, have I inscribed these simple lays
To thee, my brother, and to auld lang syne.

The rolling years have thinned our locks of brown
    To a scant fleece of salt-and-pepper gray ;
    More rapidly the seasons pass away ;
    With steadier, slower beat our pulses play ;
We like the country rather than the town,

And have a strong dislike to noise and riot.
    The fire of youth no longer warms our veins ;
    And, being subject to rheumatic pains,
    We grow prophetic as to winds and rains,
And like to be well fed, well clothed, and quiet.

That we are past our youth is all too plain;

    And nearing rapidly the Dark Divide.

    Oh, passing weary is this middle tide

    Of life, which I would give, with aught beside,

To live one year of boyhood o'er again!

It may not be. The wrinkles on each face

    Are past erasure: and not many years

    Can glide ere one of us with blinding tears

    Shall stand beside the marble which uprears

Above a friend the world can not replace.

"NESSMUK."

It is a sad necessity that compels a man to speak often or much of himself. Most writers come to loathe the first person singular, and to look upon the capital *I* as a pronominal calamity. And yet, how can a man tell aught of himself without the "eternal ego?"

I am led to these remarks by a request of my publishers that I furnish some account of myself in issuing this little volume of verse. Readers who take an interest in the book will, as a rule, wish to know something of the Author's antecedents, they think. It might also be thought that the man who has spent a large share of the summer and autumn months in the deep forests, and mostly alone for fifty years, ought to have a large stock of anecdote and adventure to draw on.

It is not so certain, this view of it. The average person is slow to understand how utterly monotonous and lonely is a life in the depths of a primal forest, even to the most incorrigible hunter. Few city sportsmen will believe, without practical observation, that a man may hunt faithfully in an unbroken forest for an entire week without getting a single shot, and one wet week, especially if it be cold and stormy, is usually enough to disgust him who has traveled hundreds of miles for an outing at much outlay of time and money.

And yet, this is a common experience of the most ardent still hunter.

In the gloomy depths of an unbroken forest there is seldom a song bird to be heard. The absence of small game is remarkable ; and the larger animals, deer, bears, and panthers, are scarce and shy. In such a forest I have myself hunted faithfully from Monday morning till Saturday night, from daylight until dark each day, and at the end of the last day brought the old double-barreled muzzle loader into camp with the same bullets in the gun that I drove home on the first morning. And I crept stealthily through the thickets in still-hunting moccasins on the evening of the last day with as much courage and enjoyment as on the first morning. For I knew that, sooner or later, the supreme moment would come, when the black, satiny coat of a bear, or the game-looking " short-blue " coat of a buck would, for an instant, offer fair for the deadly bead.

And once, in a dry, noisy, Indian summer time, I am ashamed to say, I still-hunted 17 days without getting one shot at a deer. It was the worst luck I ever had, but I enjoyed the weather and the solitary camp-life. At last there came a soft November rain, the rustling leaves became like a wet rug, and the nights were pitch dark. Then the deer came forth from swamps and laurel brakes, the walking was almost noiseless, and I could kill all I could take care of.

It is only the born woods crank who can enjoy going to the depths of a lonely forest with a heavy rifle and stinted rations, season after season, to camp alone for weeks at a stretch, in a region as dreary and desolate as—Broadway on a summer afternoon in May.

It is only the descendants of Ananias who are always meeting with hair-breadth escapes and startling adventures on their hunting trips. To the practical, skilled woodsman, their wonderful stories bear the plain imprint of lies. He knows that the deep forest is more safe than the most orderly town ; and that there is more danger in meeting one " bridge gang " than there would be in meeting all the wild animals in New York or Pennsylvania.

These facts will explain why I have so little to relate in the way of adventure, though my aggregate of camp-life, most of it alone, will foot up at least 12 years.

I can scarcely recall a dozen adventures from as many years' outings, culled from the cream of fifty seasons. Incidents of woods life, and interesting ones, are of almost daily occurrence ; and these, to the ardent lover of nature, form the attraction of forest life in a far greater degree than does the brutal love of slaughter for the mere pleasure of killing something just because it is alive.

Just here my literary Mentor and Stentor, who has been coolly going through my MSS., remarks sententiously, " Better throw this stuff into the stove and start off with your biography. That is what the Editor wants." I answer vaguely, " Story ? Lord bless you ; I have none to tell, sir. Alas ! there is so little in an ordinary, humdrum life that is worth the telling. And there is such a wilderness of biographies and autobiographies that no one cares to read."

" Well, you've agreed to do it, you know, and no one is obliged to read it. It will make ' filling ' any how ; and probably that's all the Editor wants." Which is complimentary and encouraging.

" I must say it's the toughest job of penwork I ever tackled : I don't know how to begin."

" Pooh ! Begin in the usual way. Say you were born in the town of —"

" There's where you're out. I wasn't born in any town what-ever, but in what New Englanders call a ' gore ' — a triangu-lar strip of land that gets left out somehow when the towns are surveyed. They reckon it in, however, when it comes to taxes ; but it rather gets left on schools."

" Ah, I can believe it. Well, fix it up to suit yourself. I suppose the Editor keeps a ' balaam box.' "

Taking his leave and a handful of my Lone-Jack, C. saunters off to the village, and I am left to myself. Perhaps his advice is good. Let's see how it will work on a send-off. For instance, I was born in a sterile part of sterile Massachusetts, on the border of Douglas Woods, within half a mile of Nepmug Pond, and within three miles of Junkamaug Lake. This startling event happened in the " South Gore," about 64 years ago. I did not have a fair average start in life at first. A snuffy old nurse who was present at my birth was fond of telling me in after years a legend like this : " Ga-a-rge, you on'y weighed fo' pounds when you wuz born, 'n' we put ye inter a quart mug 'n' turned a sasser over ye."

I could have killed her, but I didn't. Though I was glad when she died, and assisted at her funeral with immense satisfaction.

Junkamaug Lake is six miles long, with many bays, points, and islands, with dense thickets along its shores at the time of which I speak, and a plentiful stock of pickerel, perch and other fish. It was just the sort of country to delight the Indian mind ; and here it was that a remnant of the Nepmug Indians had a reservation, while they also had a camp on the shores of Nepmug Pond, where they spent much time, loafing, fishing, making baskets, and setting snares for rabbits and grouse. They were a disreputable gang of dirty, copper-colored vagabonds, with little notion of responsibility or decency, and too lazy even to hunt.

There were a few exceptions, however. Old Ja-ha was past 90, and the head man of the gang. He really had a deal of the old-time Indian dignity ; but it was all thrown away on that band of shiftless reprobates. There were two or three young squaws, suspiciously light of complexion, but finely formed and of handsome features. " I won't go bail for any thing beyond."

The word Nepmuk, or, as it is sometimes spelled, Nepmug, means Wood-duck. This, in the obsolete lingo of the once powerful Narragansetts. The best Indian of the band was " Injun Levi," as the whites called him. He was known among his tribe as " Nessmuk ;" and I think he exerted a stronger influence on my future than any other man. As a fine physical specimen of the animal man I have seldom seen his equal. As a woodsman and a trusty friend he was good as gold ; but he could not change the Indian nature that throbbed in every vein and filled his entire being. Just here I can not do better than reproduce a sketch of him and his tribe which appeared in the columns of *Forest and Stream* in December,

1881. I will add that Junkamaug is only a corruption of the
Indian name, and the other names I give as I had them from the
Indians themselves :

" * * * And I remain yours sincerely, NESSMUK, which
means in the Narragansett tongue, or did mean, as long as
there were any Narragansetts to give tongue, Wood-duck, or
rather, Wood-drake.

"Also, it was the name of the athletic young brave, who was
wont to steal me away from home before I was five years old,
and carry me around Nepmug and Junkamaug lakes, day after
day, until I imbibed much of his woodcraft, all his love for
forest life, and alas, much of his good-natured shiftlessness.

"Even now my blood flows faster as I think of the rides I
had on his well-formed shoulders, a little leg on either side of
his neck, and a death-grip on his strong, black mane ; or rode,
'belly-bumps,' on his back across old Junkamaug, hugging
him tightly around the neck, like a selfish little egotist that I
was. He tire ? He drown ? I would as soon have thought to
tire a wolf or drown a whale. At first, these excursions were
not fairly concluded without a final settlement at home—said
settlement consisting of a head-raking with a fine-toothed comb
that left my scalp raw, and a subsequent interview, of a private
nature, with 'Par,' behind the barn, at which a yearling apple
tree sprout was always a leading factor. (My blood tingles a
little at that recollection too.)

"Gradually they came to understand that I was incorrigible,
or, as a maiden aunt of the old school put it, 'given over ;'
and, so that I did not run away from school, I was allowed to
'run with them dirty Injuns,' as the aunt aforesaid expressed it.

"But I did run away from school, and books of the dry sort,
to study the great book of nature. Did I lose by it ? I can not
tell, even now. As the world goes, perhaps yes. No man can
transcend his possibilities.

"I am no believer in the supernatural: mesmerism, spirit-
ualism, and a dozen other 'isms are, to me, but as fetish. But,
I sometimes ask myself, did the strong, healthy, magnetic

nature of that Indian pass into my boyish life, as I rode on his powerful shoulders, or slept in his strong arms beneath the soft whispering pines of 'Douglas Woods?'

"Poor Nessmuk! Poor Lo! Fifty years ago the remnant of that tribe numbered thirty-six, housed, fed and clothed by the state. The same number of Dutchmen, under the same conditions, would have over-run the state ere this.

"The Indians have passed away forever; and, when I tried to find the resting place of my old friend, with the view of putting a plain stone above his grave, no one could point out the spot.

"And this is how I happen to write over the name by which he was known among his people, and the reason why a favorite dog or canoe is quite likely to be called Nessmuk."

The foregoing will partly explain how it came that, ignoring the weary, devious roads by which men attain to wealth and position, I became a devotee of nature in her wildest and roughest aspects—a lover of field sports—a hunter, angler, trapper, and canoeist—an uneducated man, withal, save the education that comes of long and close communion with nature, and a perusal of the best English authors.

Endowed by nature with an instinctive love of poetry, I early dropped into the habit of rhyming. Not with any thought or ambition to become a poet; but because at times a train of ideas would keep waltzing through my head in rhyme and rhythm like a musical nightmare, until I got rid of measure and metre by transferring them to paper, or, as more than once happened, to white birch bark, when paper was not to be had.

I never yet sat down with malice .prepense to rack and wrench my light mental machinery for the evolution of a poem through a rabid desire for literary laurel. On the contrary, much of the best verse I have ever written has gone to loss through being penciled on damp, whitey-brown paper or birch bark, in woodland camps or on canoeing cruises, and then rammed loosely into a wet pocket or knapsack, to turn up illegible or missing when wanted. When

> "I looked in unlikely places
> Where lost things are sure to be found,"

and found them not, I said, all the better for my readers, if I ever have any. Let them go with the thistle-down, far a-lee. (The rhymes, not the readers.)

I trust that the sparrow-hawks of criticism, who delight equally in eulogising laureates and scalping linnets, will deal gently with an illiterate backwoodsman who ventures to plant his moccasins in the realms of rhyme. Maybe they will pass me by altogether, as

> "A literary tomtit, the chickadee of song."

There must be a few graybeards left who remember Nessmuk through the medium of *Porter's Spirit of the Times*, in the long ago fifties ; and many more who have come to regard him kindly as a contributor to *Forest and Stream*. If it happens that a thousand or so of these have a curiosity to see what sort of score an old woodsman can make as an off-hand, short-range poet, it will be a complimentary feather in the cap of the author,

WELLSBORO, Pa., Oct. 9th, 1886. GEO. W. SEARS.

CONTENTS.

MY ATTIC,

CRAGS AND PINES,
   Stalking a Buck,
   Hunting Song,
   A Summer Camp,
   Sunrise in the Forest,
   October,
   New Year's Eve in Camp,
   Lotos Eating,
   My Forest Camp,
   My Hound,
   Mickle Run Falls,
   A Fragment,
   Our Camping Ground,
   Watching the River,
   Flight of the Goddess,
   On the Death of Buffie,
   Why I Love Hiawatha,
   That Trout,
   Breaking Camp,

MY NEIGHBOR OVER THE WAY,
   Pauper Plaint,
   John O' the Smithy,
   The Doers,

Surly Joe's Christmas,   65

The Genius Loci of Wall Street,   67

From the Misanthrope,   69

Gleaning After the Fire,   81

Lines for the Times,   83

Drawers and Hewers,   86

Disheartened,   89

The Smiths,   91

To John Bull on his Christmas,   93

OUR LITTLE PRINCE,   95

It Does not Pay,   97

The Hunter's Lament,   99

Ida May,   102

Ione,   103

All Things Come Round,   105

My Woodland Princess,   107

Remembered—L. K.,   109

Mother and Child,   110

Bessie Irelan,   112

A Little Grave,   114

A Summer Night,   116

Wreck of the Gloucester,   118

Haste,   119

A Christmas Entry,   120

Two Lives,   122

Elaine,   124

Anna Fay—on Skates,   125

Paraphrase on "Brahma,"   128

The Retired Preacher,   129

Waiting for Her Prince,   132

May,   135

Isabel Nye,   136

Deacon John,   138

Hannah Lee,   141

At Anchor,   143

The Cavan Girl,   145

Old Johnny Jones,   146

IN THE TROPICS, -   147

The Mameluco Dance,   151

A Tropical Scrap,   161

Typee,   162

To Gen. T. L. Young,   164

Roses of Imeeo, -   167

A Dream of the Tropics,   168

Desilusano,   170

AN ARKANSAS IDYL,   172

The Scalp Hunter is Interviewed,   177

The Banshee of McBride,   181

How Miah Jones got Discouraged,   186

GREETING TO THE DEAD,   188

New Year's Ode.—1866, -   189

Ballad of ye Leek Hook,   191

King Cotton,   193

Non Respondat,   194

Sixty-five and John Bull, -   196

New Year's Ode,   199

CRUSADING THE OLD SALOON,   202

Temperance Song,   206

O'Leary's Lament,   208

Wellsboro as a Temperance Town, -   209

MY ATTIC.

I HAVE an attic—not city made,
   Nor far removed from the fresh green earth,
Strewn with the tools of a manly trade,
   And guns, and fiddles, and books of worth.

A narrow window looks toward the town,
   Where, shown by waves of the summer breeze,
Are checkered glimpses of white and brown,
   Peeping thro' maple and linden trees.

A little brook that murmurs and flows,
   A little garden of well tilled land,
And trees, not standing in stiff, straight rows,
   All planted and pruned by the owner's hand,

Lovingly tended, thriftily grown,
   With many a quaint, odd crook and trend
I know their names as I know my own,
   And every tree is a personal friend.

At the first faint glimmer on rock and tree
   I rise, with the earliest blue-birds' trill.
'Tis a freak of mine ; and I like to see
   The sunshine break on Losinger Hill ;

For I like him best in his morning face,
   Untired with the daily race he runs;
And I'm sometimes sad when he yields his place
   To the winds of night and the lesser suns.

I ply the thread and the brightened awl
   To the runes that the woodland thrushes sing;
And the plash of a tiny waterfall
   Keeps merry time to the lapstone's ring.

And little I reck, as I shape the sole,
   Of scanty clothing or empty purse,
I sing the ballad of old King Cole,
   Or wear my leisure on simple verse.

The man of millions shall pass away,
   His wealth divided, himself forgot,
But better one leaf of deathless bay
   Than all the riches that rust and rot.

And at rare, odd times, in the better moods,
   Some rustic verses to me are born,
That may live, perchance, in their native woods
   As long as the crows that pull the corn.

CRAGS AND PINES.

WHO treads the dirty lanes of trade
    Shall never know the wondrous things
  Told by the rugged forest kings
To him who sleeps beneath their shade.

Only to him whose coat of rags
    Has pressed at night their royal feet
    Shall come the secrets, strange and sweet,
Of regal pines and beetling crags.

For him the Wood-nymph shall unlock
    The mystic treasures which have lain
    A thousand years, in frost and rain,
Deep in the bosom of the rock.

For this and these he must lay down
    The things that worldlings most do prize,
    Holding his being in her eyes,
His fealty to her laurel crown.

No greed of gold shall come to him,
   Nor strong desire of earthly praise ;
   But he shall love the silent ways
Of forest aisles and arches dim.

And dearer hold the open page
   Of nature's book than shrewdest plan
   By which man cheats his fellow man,
Or robs the workman of his wage.

STALKING A BUCK.

RESTING on leaves of feathery pine,
    Stilling my lurcher's eager whine,
Stealthy and watchful I recline.

Gray streaks are in the eastern sky :
The morning breeze floats gently by,
And all alert of hand or eye

I watch the mist rise o'er the stream.
Slowly athwart the copses gleam
Bright streaks of sunlight ; and one beam

Dashes against the wrinkled crag
Where, mid the ferns and brake and rag-
Wort, feeds alone a gallant stag.

A hundred rods I needs must pass
Through brake, and thorn, and rank wet grass,
O'er fallen logs and deep morass.

A clump of briars is gained unseen.
Cautious, above the leafy screen
I raise my head : with royal mien

And antlered brow of regal pride,
His forefeet in the rippling tide,
There stands the stag, his glossy side

Turned fairly to me.   True and fine
The sights range up in deadly line—
One sharp report—the stag is mine!

*   *   *   *   *   *   *   *

Beneath a rustic roof of bark
Idly I course each rising spark,
Limned on the hemlocks grim and dark.

Red steaks are broiling, sweet and slow,
And in the camp-fire's ruddy glow
A crystal streamlet sings below.

My lurcher, crouching at my side,
In very joy and canine pride
Keeps watch upon the antlered hide.

Oh, for a heaven wherein the deer,
Shall be more plentiful than here—
And brown October all the year!

HUNTING SONG.

THE lovers of mammon but treasure up wrath,
There's a specter that follows in glory's red path :
A curse ever follows the gripers of gold,
And the hearts of fame-seekers are callous and cold.

I will build me a camp by a cool mountain spring,
Where the trout play at eve and the wood thrushes sing ;
I will roof it with bark ; and my snug sylvan house
Shall be sweet with the fragrance of evergreen boughs.

When the shadows of night settle down on the marsh,
And the cry of the bittern booms sullen and harsh,
The glow of my camp-fire shall glisten and shine
Where the beech and the hemlock their branches entwine.

When a boy, 'twas my chiefest of pleasures to make
A rude camp in the forest, by river or lake,
Where the rod and the rifle induced through the day
The fatigue that at night passed so sweetly away.

There were freshness and joy past the power of words
In the crisp morning air and the voices of birds ;
And 'twas sweet into slumber at night to decline
By the low alto song of the evergreen pine.

A SUMMER CAMP.

THE sun is savage in sultry hollows,
  The hillside quivers with pulsing heat.
With drooping wings the dusty swallows
  Are dotting the fence that lines the street.

I leave the town with its hundred noises,
  Its clatter and whir of wheel and steam,
For woodland quiet and silvery voices,
  With a camp of bark by a crystal stream.

Oh, shrewd are the ways of town and city,
  Cunning in commerce and worldly wise,
But hearts grow hardened to human pity,
  And tongues slop over with thrifty lies.

Nearer to Him of the lowly manger
  Is the sun-tanned forester, broad and free,
And the rugged hills in their native grandeur
  Are nearer the hills of Galilee.

The feathery arms of firs and spruces
  Bend over the water that sleeps beneath,
Where marish flowers by the quiet sluices
  Infold their sweets in a golden sheath.

And a small canoe of airy lightness
  Floats silently on the limpid stream,
Where the norland birch in snowy whiteness
  O'erhangs the ripples that glance and gleam.

Oh, peaceful and sweet are forest slumbers
  On a fragrant couch with the stars above,
As the free soul marches to dulcet numbers
  Through dreamland valleys of light and love.

And ever at night a sylvan goddess
  Glides into my camp with dance and song :
In kirtle of green and snowy bodice
  She stays by my side the whole night long.

She cools my forehead with dainty fingers,
  And smooths the wrinkles from brow and face
With a pitying touch that clings and lingers
  About my spirit in every place.

On emerald banks thick strewn with pansies
  We loiter away the dreamy days,
And she dowers my soul with sylvan fancies
  That sprout and blossom in rustic lays.

Why should I envy the laureate guinea,
  Or covet the muse that is held in fief ?
I sing the ballads she prompts within me,
  And have no spite for the greener leaf.

With luckier bards I have no quarrel,

    I envy no brow its wreath of bays :

I know it is mine to miss the laurel,

    And the golden sheen of the leaf that pays,

And I rest in the hope that each good fellow

    Will some time dwell in another land,

Where hearts that are generous, true and mellow,

    Will know each other, and understand.

———

SUNRISE IN THE FOREST.

THE zephyrs of morning are stirring the larches,

    And, lazily lifting, the mist rolls away.

A pæan of praise thro' the dim forest arches

    Is ringing, to welcome the advent of day.

        Is loftily ringing,

        Exultingly ringing,

From the height where a little brown songster is clinging,

    The top of a hemlock, the uttermost spray.

OCTOBER.

BY A STILL-HUNTER.

THERE comes a month in the weary year,
   A month of leisure and peaceful rest,
When the ripe leaves fall and the air is clear —
   October, the brown, the crisp, the blest.

My lot has little enough of bliss ;
   I drag the days of the odd eleven —
Counting the time that shall lead to this,
   The month that opens the hunter's heaven.

And oh, for the mornings crisp and white,
   With the sweep of the hounds upon the track :
The bark-roofed cabins, the camp-fire's light,
   The break of the deer and the rifle's crack.

Do you call this trifling ?   I tell you, friend,
   A life in the forest is past all praise.
Give me a dozen such months on end —
   You may take my balance of years and days.

For brick and mortar breed filth and crime,
　　And a pulse of evil that throbs and beats.
And men are withered before their prime
　　By the curse paved in with the lanes and streets.

And lungs are poisoned, and shoulders bowed,
　　In the smothering reek of mill and mine ;
And death stalks in on the struggling crowd —
　　But he shuns the shadow of oak and pine.

And of all to which the memory clings,
　　There is naught so dear as the sunny spots
Where our shanties stood by the crystal springs,
　　The vanished hounds and the lucky shots.

MARCH 16, 1868.

NEW YEAR'S EVE IN CAMP.

MERCURY 10° BELOW ZERO, NORTHWEST GALE.

THE winds are out in force to-night, the clouds, in light
  brigades,
Are charging from the mountain tops across the everglades.
There is a fierceness in the air—a dull, unearthly light—
The Frost-king in his whitest crown rides on the storm to-night.
Far down the gorge of Otter Run I hear the sullen roar
Of rifted snows and pattering sleet, among the branches hoar.
The giant hemlocks wag their heads against the midnight sky,
The melancholy pine trees moan, the cedars make reply.

The oaks and sugar maples toss their frozen arms in air,
The elms and beeches bow their heads, and shriek as in despair.
Scant shield to-night for flesh and blood is feather, hair, or fur:
From north to south, for many a mile, there is no life astir.

The gaudy jay with painted crest has stowed his plumes away,
The sneaking wolf forbears to howl, the mountain cat to prey.
The deer has sought the laurel brake, her form the timid hare,
The shaggy bear is in his den, the panther in his lair.

From east to west, from north to south, for twenty miles around,
To-night no track shall dint the shroud that wraps the frozen
      ground.

I sit and listen to the storm that roars and swells aloof,
Watching the fitful shadows play against the rustic roof,
And as I blow an idle cloud to while the hours away,
I croon an old-time ditty, in the minor key of A.

And from the embers beams a face most exquisitely fair—
The maiden face of one I knew—no matter when or where,
A face inscrutable and calm, with dark, reproachful eyes,
That gaze on me from limpid depths, or gusty autumn skies.

And there may be a reason why I shun the blatant street,
To seek a distant mountain glen where three bright waters meet.
But why I shun the doors of men, their rooms a-light and warm,
To camp in forest depths alone, or face a winter storm,
Or why the heart that gnaws itself will find relief in rhyme,
I cannot tell: I but abide the footing up of Time.

LOTOS EATING.

WHEN nor'west winds with sullen roar
   Swept round the ricks and stables,
When winter, beaten off before,
   Began to turn the tables,
When all was snug in barn and byre,
   When autumn rains were pouring,
When bairns were ranting round the fire
   That up the lug was roaring,

Then said our melancholy Jacques,
   As he his soles was heating,
" Let's lay aside the plow and ax—
   I go for lotos eating."
"Oh ho," said Fritz, with smiling phiz,
   " You've read to your confusion.
You ought to know the lotos is
   An Eastern institution.

"No doubt its powers are past belief—
   I'd like to taste the lotos.
But you will scarcely find the leaf
   Among our hardy voters."

Jacques hummed the Lass o' Balloch myle :
　　Said he, " It's immaterial,
And let us take a friendly smile—
　　Pass round the liquid cereal."

(We took our rye in liquid form.)
　　So each drank off his liquor,
The while outside the driving storm
　　Grew heavier and thicker.
We spread a bearskin on the floor
　　And roused the sparkling fire,
Then latched and barred the shaking door,
　　For still the wind rose higher.

With coat and overcoat and vest
　　We improvised three couches,
Then stretched our lazy limbs in rest,
　　And drew our pipes and pouches.
And as we blew an idle cloud
　　The while the storm was beating,
Said Jacques, " I'll leave it to the crowd
　　That *this* is lotos eating."

MY FOREST CAMP.

I HAVE a camp in Yarnel Glen,
  A hunter's cabin, roofed with bark,
Far from the noisy haunts of men,
  Where song of thrush or meadow lark
Floats never on the somber air.
  When summer suns are fiercely hot
And birds sit mute with drooping wing,
  Ofttimes I seek this lonely spot,
My cabin by the mountain spring,
  And spend my days of leisure there.

Perchance some book of pleasant vein
  May wile an hour of idle time.
Perchance I choose the quaint refrain
  Of Chaucer or of Spenser's rhyme,
  Nor heed the failing day's decline.
At night my forest bed I make
  On fragrant boughs, and sweetly dream
Of deer or trout that I may take
  On mountain side or forest stream,
With rifle true or silken line.

When autumn frosts have clothed the woods
   In hues of gold and crimson red,
Again I seek these solitudes,
   The moss-grown spring and forest bed.
Again I breathe the mountain air.
   Then give me but my forest home,
My rifle, rod, and buoyant health,
   With freedom where I please to roam ;
And take who will the banker's wealth,
   His sleepless nights of anxious care.

MY HOUND.

I HAVE wandered far in many a clime,
    And many a faithful friend have found,
But done who better deserves my rhyme
    Than brave old Nigger, my faithful hound;
For never a man on land or sea
Had truer ally or friend than he.

His coat is sleek as an Arab steed,
    He is clean of limb as a yearling deer.
A match for the greyhound in his speed,
    With a voice so loud and silvery clear
You would swear, as he sweeps thro' the mountain dells,
'Twas a musical chime of vesper bells.

Often, when tired of this strife for bread,
    Have he and I wandered where gurgling rills
In purity spring from their mountain bed
    In the ice-cold bosoms of distant hills;
And, leaving the world to its wearisome ways,
Have built us a shanty and camped for days.

And often when night closed over our camp
   And he was away on the track of deer,
Have I breathless listened to catch the tramp
   Of his pattering feet draw swiftly near.
.I have listened till silence became a pain,
But never yet did I listen in vain.

I have lain by my camp-fire's glowing light
   And lazily fingered his silken ears,
Till meeting his eye, so wistfully bright,
   My own has silently filled with tears
As I thought with shame of some harsh rebuff
To my poor dumb friend, when my mood was rough.

MICKLE RUN FALLS.

FRONT-FACING the east, where the Falls are down
        pouring,
  A fairy like rainbow is formed on the spray.
Beneath it the waters are rushing and roaring
  To the pool, where by moonlight the brown otters play,
Are rushing and roaring, are dashing and roaring,
Away to the vale where the eagle is soaring,
  And the blue Susquehanna sweeps down to the bay.

By the point of the rocks, at the foot of the mountain,
  Foaming over a boulder moss-covered and gray,
Is bubbling and gushing a crystalline fountain
  Where the red deer are browsing the long summer day.
Are daintily browsing, are warily browsing,
Above the deep pool where the trout are carousing,
  And the slide of the otter is moist with the spray.

A FRAGMENT.

OH, leave this chase for place or gold
   Through legal quips and tangles,
Which makes young eyes grow hard and cold,
   With crowsfeet at the angles.

The miser's hoard but pays his board,
   With meager clothes and bedding,
While oft he finds a golden road
   Exceedingly hard sledding.

Then come, ye dwellers of the town,
   From shop, and lane, and alley,
To where a river sparkles down
   A hemlock shaded valley.

Take from your life one week of strife,
   And add a week of leisure,
That memory may some future day
   Fall back upon with pleasure.

OUR CAMPING GROUND.

THERE is a spot where plumy pines
  O'erhang the sylvan banks of Otter,
Where pigeons feed among the vines
  That hang above the limpid water.
There wood-ducks build in hollow trees,
  And herns among the matted sedges,
While, drifting on the summer breeze,
  Float satin clouds with silver edges

'Tis there the blue jay hides her nest
  In thickest shade of drooping beeches,
The fish-hawk, statue-like in rest,
  Stands guard o'er glassy pools and reaches.
The trout beneath the grassy brink
  Looks out for shipwrecked flies and midges,
The red deer comes in search of drink,
  From laurel brake and woodland ridges.

And on the stream a birch canoe
  Floats like a freshly fallen feather—
A fairy thing, that will not do
  For broader seas or stormy weather.

The sides no thicker than the shell
  Of Ole Bull's Cremona fiddle—
The man who rides it will do well
  To part his scalplock in the middle.

Beneath a hemlock grim and dark,
  Where shrub and vine are intertwining,
Our shanty stands, well roofed with bark,
  On which the cheerful blaze is shining.
The smoke ascends in spiral wreath,
  With upward curve the sparks are trending,
The coffee kettle sings beneath
  Where smoke and sparks and leaves are blending.

Upon the whole this life is well :
  Our lines are cast in pleasant places.
And it is better not to dwell
  On missing forms and vanished faces.
They have their rest beyond our bourn ;—
  We miss the old familiar voices.
We will remember—will not mourn :
  The heart is poor that ne'er rejoices.

We had our day of youth and May,
  We may have grown a trifle sober ;
But life may reach a wintry day,
  And we are only in October.

Then here's a round to every hound
   That ran his deer by hill or hollow,
And every man who watched the ground
   From Barber Rock to Furman fallow.

WATCHING THE RIVER.

I WATCH by the river as, long ago,
   I watched by the waters of Mendon Mere.
   And what do I see, and what do I hear,
As the river goes by in endless flow?

A fishhawk, watching the glassy pools;
   A mountain, abutting upon the stream.
   An eagle, sailing with angry scream,
And trout, and minnows, in swarming schools.

A rugged vista of mountain spurs
   That crowd the river to left or right,
   Rough, granite boulders that crown the height,
And a dark green ocean of pines and firs.

And now as of old the woods are ripe
   With mystic murmur of sylvan sounds;
   For over the hill are eager hounds,
And a red deer running to win his life.

FLIGHT OF THE GODDESS.

[Answer to T. B. Aldrich's "Flight of the Goddess" in *Atlantic Monthly*, October, 1867.]

I MET your Goddess, a week ago,
  In the mountains, a mile above Elk Run.
Sitting where crystal springs out-flow
  To ripple away in shade and sun.

She sat by the spring, on a fallen log,
  Sulkily leaning against a pine.
And she welcomed me with my gun and dog —
  This sweetest maiden of all the Nine.

I was ragged enough — and so was she —
  Had we been in the city's streets to beg.
Her kirtle was rent above the knee —
  Shall I ever again see such a leg?

"She was sick of the city," so she said,
  Where all her lovers had played her false.
Leaving her Delphian board and bed,
  For an earthly maid, who could flirt and waltz.

She had treated her lovers like a queen,
  Dwelt in their attics through heat and cold ;
Cheered them in sickness ; and wasn't it mean
  To whistle her off for place or gold ?

Halleck, her lover in other days,
  Had used her worse than a heathen Turk.
Had hung in a counting room her bays,
  And taken hire as a merchant's clerk.

And as for Aldrich — perhaps he'd find
  'Twas something more than the muse would stand,
To whistle her coolly down the wind
  For a Yankee Goddess with house and land.—

I leaned the rifle against a tree,
  And knelt in the pine leaves at her feet.
I pressed my cheek to the well turned knee
  And prayed — "O Goddess, divinely sweet,

"Come with me to my hut of linden bark,
  Well strewn with the fragrant hemlock leaves.
I will be thy deer : be thou my park :
  We will rest while the lonely night bird grieves.

"I solemnly swear to never possess
  A dollar that I can call my own,
To go an-hungered and ragged in dress,
  To love forever but Thee alone."

She touched my forehead with finger tips
   That warmed like a camp-fire's ruddy glow.
I pressed the peerless hand to my lips—
   It melted away like April snow.

" Oh stay," I cried, with a feeble gasp,
   "Touch with thy sacred fire my lines."
And I strove her vanishing form to clasp,
   As she fled and faded among the pines.

And thus it comes that I love to dwell
   Afar from the clamor of busy men.
Where the crystal waters sob and swell
   To sweet, low echoes that haunt the glen.

And deep on the night I sometimes hear,
   In the soft round tops of the pines and firs,
A rhythmic cadence so low and clear
   That I know the song can be only hers.

ON THE DEATH OF BUFFIE.

A handsome young hound, with a voice like a silver bugle. He made too much noise o' nights; and there be dull souls who prefer sleep to music. Buffie was poisoned by the very man whom he had serenaded for weeks!·

PUIR BUFFIE.

After the Lallans of Burns.

GAE tell to a' the hunters roun'
    That Geordie's heart is sair cast down;
Wi' hirplin' step he treads the groun',
    An' hingin' head.
Buffie, the wale o' youthfu' houn's,
    Puir Buffie's dead.

Let ilka tod frae Butler's hill
To Allen's swamp an' Merrick's rill,
For vera joy bark loud an' shrill
    Wi' muckle glee.
Puir Buffie's lyin' stark and still
    Out owre the lea.

Had he been slain in open day
By hoof or horn o' stag at bay,
I wadna hae the heart to say
    It did him wrang:
'Tis murd'rous an' unmanly play
    That gies the pang.

Na doubt but he at times might draw
Ae sned o' beef wi' thievin' jaw,
Or, aiblins on fine nights might blaw
   About the street,
But if that faut's agin' the law,
    He couldna see't.

Perhaps he might in pleasant weather
Wi' ither tykes sometime foregather
To fyke on grocer's wares. But whether
   He did or not,
In spite o' a' their scauldin' blether's
    A triflin' faut.

He maks the fourth o' lang eared frien's
Wha followed me o'er hills an' glens
Until they met untimely ends
   By murder sair.
Their fauts were something less than men's,
    Their virtues mair.

But Buffie dog, a long fareweel !
Nae doubt ye were a roguish chiel :—
But aiblins there's anither field
   Where thou an' I
Maun chance to fin' a cantie bield
    Ayont the sky.

WHY I LOVE HIAWATHA.

A TALE.   BY CURTUS COMOS.

O F all sweet poetic meters
    That the bards have ever chanted,
From the days of old blind Homer
To the times of poet Tupper,
No one hath more pleasant chiming
Than Longfellow's Indian legend
When he sings of Hiawatha —
Of heroic Hiawatha.
Reason good have I to love it,
Reason have I to be grateful,
And thereby a tale is hanging.

THE TALE.

'Twas in frosty bright October
When the lofty sugar maples
Don their robes of golden glory,
When the graceful drooping birches
Put on lemon colored vestments,
When the walnuts or the beeches

All are garbed in russet yellow,
While the gentle, albic maples
Dress in royal robes of scarlet,
Royal robes of gorgeous scarlet ;
'Twas in brilliant hued October,
When the smoky Indian summer
Was upon the land in beauty,
When the outlines of the mountains
Seem like rolls of purple velvet,
That with tomahawk and rifle
Hied I to the primal forest —
To the grand and silent forest.

Oh the days of dreamy pleasure
    That I passed upon the mountain ;
And the nights of sleepy leisure
    In my camp beside the fountain.

Resting with my dog beside me
    Free from earthly botheration,
None to question me or chide me —
    'Twas contentment's culmination.

Summer rainbows are full pleasant
    With their hues in beauty blending,
But they vanish with the present,
    And all pleasures have an ending.

Thus it was on this occasion,
  That an idle, thoughtless fellow
Of Milesian persuasion,
  Who was fond of getting mellow,

Sought me over hill and mountain,
  Sought me ever till he found me
In my camp beside the fountain
  With my hunting kit around me.

Now, adieu to peace and quiet,
  For he hath a gallon bottle ;
And he loveth noise and riot —
  With his cursed copper throttle.

All night long the drouthy creature
  Howled and sang in his carouse,
Of the battle of "Boyne wather,"
  And the "Woman wid three cows."

Told me tales of " Ould Killarney,"
  Sang the song of " Norah Kreena,"
And, when tired of song and blarney
  Raised the deathly Irish " Keenah."

Yelling wildly, laughing gayly,
  With most impudent assurance
Flourishing a big shelala —
  It was getting past endurance.

Kept it up throughout the morrow,
 Howling like a dozen demons;
And I saw with dread and horror
 That the fellow had the tremens,

Filling me with fear and loathing,
 Loading me with foul abuse,
Seeing snakes upon his clothing,
 Rats and spiders on his shoes.

And he threatened me with murder,
Murder in the lonely forest,
Thinking that I was a rival
For the favors of his Mary:
Mary in the isle of Erin,
On the verdant banks of Shannon.
Mary, who her troth had plighted
To this drunken son of Connaught —
To this wild, red headed paddy.

And he dared me to a duel,
Dared me to a deadly duel!
Swore that I should not escape him,
But should fight him in the forest,
He, with bottle and shelala,
I, with tomahawk and rifle.

Then to save my soul from murder,
From the deadly sin of murder,
Drew I forth a pocket volume
Of the poem, Hiawatha !
Drew it forth ; and with a steady
And determined recitation ;
With a mono-tonous droning
And undaunted resolution,
Fell upon the raving paddy
With the cadence of the rhythm.

And in vain was all his striving
'Gainst the measure of the poem.
Vain was all his fierce invective,
As I poured the soothing cadence
On his wild and savage spirit.
And he wilted at the drowsy
And unceasing intonation ;
Wilted at the lethean measure
That, without remorse or pity,
Closed about him like a mantle.

And his eye grew calm and quiet ;
Calm and quiet, and no longer
Saw the rats, or snakes and spiders
In his shoes, or on his clothing,
And his knees grew weak and shaky ;
Dull and heavy grew his eyelids ;

Till, his weary legs, jack-knifing,
Gave a lurch into the shanty.
In the shanty by the fountain,
By the fountain in the forest,
In the forest old and primal;
Where this wild shock-headed paddy
Sank in weariness and weakness
On my well-worn Indian blanket.

Then I placed the little volume
Where it served him for a pillow.
Placed it where his head, recumbent,
Rested on the blessed poem
That had saved my soul from murder—
From the fearful crime of murder;
Placed it there and quickly left him
To involuntary slumber,
While I mizzled for the clearings.

Three long months I left him sleeping
In the shanty by the fountain;
But at last my spirit smote me
For the trick that I had played him,
And again I took my rifle,
Took my tomahawk and rifle,
And my way into the forest,
Trusting I might find him sober!

White hands crossed upon his bosom,
Livid lips and nose ataunto,
Red hair streaming o'er the volume,
Sleeping sweetly, snoring softly—
Such the state in which I found him.
Then his shock-head I uplifted
And withdrew the little volume
Of the poem, Hiawatha!

Stirred he quickly in his slumber,
Then with gasp and snort awakened,
Sat on end, with eyes wild glaring,
Shook his red mane like a lion,
And roared out in tones of thunder:
"Holy Mither! Where's the botthle?"

THAT TROUT.

I 'VE watched that trout for days and days,
    I've tried him with all sorts of tackle ;
With flies got up in various ways,
    Red, blue, green, gray, and silver-hackle.

I've tempted him with angle-dogs,
    And grubs, that must have been quite trying,
Thrown deftly in betwixt old logs,
    Where, probably, he might be lying.

Sometimes I've had a vicious bite,
    And as the silk was tautly running,
Have been convinced I had him, quite :
    But 'twasn't him : *he* was too cunning.

I've tried him, when the silver moon
    Shone on my dew-bespangled trowsers,
With dartfish ; but he was "too soon "—
    Though, sooth to say, I caught some rousers ;

And sadly viewed the ones I caught,
   They loomed so small and seemed so poor,
'Twas finding pebbles where one sought
   A gem of price—a Kohinoor.

I've often weighed him (with my eyes),
   As he with most prodigious flounces
Rose to the surface after flies.
   (He weighs four pounds and seven ounces.)

I tried him—Heaven absolve my soul—
   With some outlandish, heathenish gearing—
A pronged machine stuck on a pole—
   A process that the boys call spearing.

I jabbed it at his dorsal fin
   Six feet beneath the crystal water—
'Twas all too short.   I tumbled in,
   And got half drowned—just as I'd orter.

Adieu, O trout of marvelous size,
   Thou piscatorial speckled wonder.
Bright be the waters where you rise,
   And green the banks you cuddle under.

BREAKING CAMP.

(OLD STYLE.)

FAREWELL to our camp on the banks of the Eddy,
 Where we frightened the herons with laughter and song.
Our skiff is hauled up and the knapsacks are ready—
 Our whiskey runs short, and the journey is long.
            The captain complains
            That it constantly rains,
And swears he prefers a secession attack.
            For each rheumatic pain
            Makes it hard to abstain
From crooking his elbow—to straighten his back.

Farewell to the spot where the doe came to water,
 And passed us in camp with the speed of the wind.
(If I wanted to lie I would say that we shot her.)
 Farewell to the hounds that came limping behind.
            Farewell to the camp
            With its earwigs and damp,
Its mountains and valleys, too rugged for use,
            Where each tramp after fish
            Made us ardently wish
We had gone in more freely for cereal juice.

Our flies were the finest, our hooks were the Kirby—
  But trout wouldn't rise with the water so high.
And 'tis strange—but 'tis true—that the captain and Derby
  The more they got wet, were more thoroughly dry!
       Farewell to the gnats
       That could bite through our hats,
  To savage musquitoes, and punkies and rain;
       To the bright-flashing spires
       That went up from our fires,
  Till we camp on the banks of the Eddy again.

    JUNE, 1869.

MY ·NEIGHBOR OVER THE WAY.

I KNOW where an old philosopher dwells,
  A bearded cynic, of wit and sense,
In a broad white web, with curious cells,
  On the sunny side of the garden fence.
He passes the days in virtuous ease,
  Watching the world with his many eyes;
And I think he is sorry when he sees
  How his web entangles the moths and flies.

I have a neighbor, a legal man—
  We meet on the sidewalk every day.
(He is shrewd to argue and scheme and plan,
  Is my legal neighbor over the way.)
He talks, perhaps, a trifle too much—
  But he knows such a vast deal more than I.
We have in our village a dozen such,
· Who do no labor—the Lord knows why.

But they eat and drink of the very best,
  And the cloth that they wear is soft and fine;
And they have more money than all the rest,
  With handsome houses, and plate, and wine.

And I ponder at times when tired and lame,
How strangely the gifts of fortune fall,
And wonder if we are not to blame,
Who have so little, yet pay for all.

Alas for the workmen over the land,
Who labor and watch, but wait too long,
Who wear the vigor of brain and hand
On trifling pleasures, and drink, and song.
Alas for the strength too much diffused,
And the lights that lure from the better way,
For the gifts and riches we have not used,
And the true hearts beating to swift decay.

Alas for the twig, perversely bent,
And the tree of knowledge, to wrong inclined;
Alas that a dollar was ever spent
Until the dollar was earned or mined.—
But my neighbor is one who understands
All social riddles; and he explains
That some must labor with calloused hands,
While others may work with tongues and brains.

Though he doesn't make it so very clear
Why he should fare much better than one
Who does more work in a single year
Than he in all of his life has done.

But he argues me out of all demur
　With logic that fogs my common sense,
And I think of the old philosopher,
　Whose "shingle" hangs by the garden fence.

PAUPER PLAINT.

WEAK and weary, tattered and torn,
　　Knees and elbows bare to the blast,—
Of all ambition and spirit shorn,
　　Beaten at last.

A dreary way is poverty's road,
　A dreary path was the bitter past.
We cry relief from the galling load,
　　Beaten at last.

The creeds and dogmas are priestly lies,
　Into the teeth of the people cast.
And thence it comes that the good, the wise,
　　Are beaten at last.

We labored while life was in its morn,
　Now we are old we faint and fast.
We have the husks—but out of the corn
　　Are beaten at last.

JOHN O' THE SMITHY.

D OWN in the vale where the mavis sings
 And the brook is turning an old-time wheel,
From morning till night the anvil rings
 Where John O' the Smithy is forging steel.
My lord rides out at the castle gate,
 My lady is grand in bower and hall,
With men and maidens to cringe and wait,
 And John O' the Smithy must pay for all.

The bishop rides in his coach and four,
 His grooms and horses are fat and sleek;
He has lackeys behind and lackeys before,
 He rides at a hundred guineas a week.
The anvil is singing its "ten pound ten,"
 The mavis pipes from his birken spray,
And this is the song that fills the glen,
 John O' the Smithy has all to pay.

The smith has a daughter, rosy and sweet,
 My lord has a son with a wicked eye:
When she hears the sound of his horses' feet
 Her heart beats quicker—she knows not why.

She will know very well before the end ;
  She will learn to detest their rank and pride,
When she has the young lord's babe to tend,
  While the bishop's daughter becomes his bride.

There will be the old, old story to tell
  Of wrong and sorrow in places high.
A bishop glozing the deeds of hell,
  The Priest and the Levite passing by.
And the father may bow his frosted head
  When he sees the young bride up at the hall,
And say 'twere better his child were dead.
  But John O' the Smithy must pay for all.

The smith and his daughter will pass away,
  And another shall make the anvil ring
For his daily bread and the hodden gray ;
  But the profits shall go to priest and king.
And over the wide world, day by day,
  The smiths shall waken at early morn,
Each to his task in the old dull way,
  To tread a measure of priestly corn.

And the smith shall live on the coarsest fare
  With little that he may call his own,
While the idler is free from work or care ;
  For the best of all must go to the drone.

And the smith complains of the anvil's song,
　　Complains of the years he has wrought and pined.
For priests and rulers are swift to wrong
　　And the mills of God are slow to grind.

But a clear strong voice from over the sea
　　Is piercing the murk of the moral night!
Time is, time was; and time shall be
　　That John O' the Smithy will have his right.
And they who have worn the miter and crown,
　　Who have pressed him sore in body and soul,
Shall perish from earth when the grist is ground
　　And the mighty miller has claimed his toll.

THE DOERS.

I SEE them ever before me, in street, in alley or lane.
   In seething slums of the city, where silent miseries lurk.
The faces of grim endurance, the eyes of stoical pain,
   The stiffened muscles of labor, the rounded shoulders of
      work.

Sweepers away of forests, workers of all that is wrought,
   Delvers in mine and workshop, Doers of all that is done.
Lacking in effort never, all too meager of thought :
   Builders and winners of all that is built or won.

Temple, cathedral or war-ship, pyramid, fortress or town,
   These have they modeled and molded, then sank to for-
      gotten graves,
Furnishing food for the battles that come of miter and crown,
   To perish by generations, like serial waves.

They form in the early morning, at the shriek of the demon
      steam,
   To march in the ranks of labor, with dull, mechanical tread ;
They delve in the grimy work-shops like men in a weary dream.
   Alas, for the lifelong battle, whose bravest slogan is bread !

The earth is teeming with fullness that springs from the Doers'
hand,
And a little bird is singing, from the roof of a western grange,
A strong heart-stirring epic, that rings throughout the land,
And the burden of all his song is only change.

SURLY JOE'S CHRISTMAS.

YOUR holidays are naught to me.
I do not care to hear or see
Your jangling bells, or Christmas tree.

With sad, dull eyes I watch the fire
On Yule logs, having no desire
For flame or fame that rises higher.

A discontented, dull content,
Much pain with little pleasure blent:
I wonder where the summer went.

Creed follows creed, fools follow fools;
Laws break through laws, rules alter rules,
Myths breed a myth, schools gender schools.

And laws, and myths, and clashing creeds
With rules and schools, and all that breeds
Discord, what are they to our needs?

Nothing.   An empty, weary sound:
The howling of a prisoned hound:
A mirage, hiding fertile ground.

A whistling wind, whose tones escape
By cornice, eaves, or gabled cape,—
Intoned by architectural shape.

THE GENIUS LOCI OF WALL STREET.

DOWN in a wonderful city, near to the foulest slums,
　Where squalor and crime are rife, and the tide flows
　　turgid and green,
Where all are greedy and blatant, where peacefulness never
　　comes,
　There squats a ravening reptile, Arachne, the Spider Queen.

After the ways of the spider, her progeny crowd her back,
　Rest on her bristly thorax, or cling to her mottled sides.
Only the wealth of a nation contents the ravenous pack,
　The fat of the land, with the commerce of all the tides.

Her throne is a street in the city, by the senseless name of
　　Wall,
　Her prey is human muscle, with the products of honest toil.
She works in her dark recesses, weaving an iron thrall,
　To steal the fruits of labor, and rob the gifts of the soil.

Her web is a net of iron that covers the plundered land,
　Entangling the plow and harrow, enthralling the ax and
　　loom.
And the well-earned profits of labor, that slip through the
　　workman's hand
　Are stored at last in the spider's den of gloom.

She sends her numerous offspring, with plausible lies to tell,
  Far out on the Nation's vineyards, while fields are of vivid
    green.
Never were men of Jewry more cunning to buy or sell,—
  And the corn and oil come back to the Spider Queen.

O men of the ocean prairie, with your sea-like fields of corn,
  How much are you the richer, for the weary years you have
    seen?
Some part has gone to the huckster, who looks on your work
  with scorn,
  But the better part to the cells of the Spider Queen.

Have you sometime thought, O toiler, when the sun was high
    and hot,
  That a nation had gone too fast, that a people might die of
    greed?
That making the land a refuge had wrought a national blot?
  That honor and strength were more than numbers or speed?

The iron web is spreading—it comes to your very door,
  It saps the sinews of labor and draws your grain from the
    sheaves.
It enters never a county but it sends a mortgage before,
  With an unseen tax that reaches from sill to eaves.

FROM THE MISANTHROPE.

WOULD that the yellow dirt, the glittering yellow dirt,
    For which men peril their lives and brave the hinges
       of hell,
Were sunk in the devil's pit where neither profit or hurt
    Could come of the heavy dross they love so well.

I am sick of the garrulous cry, the chattering, parrot cry
    Of bonds, money, and stock, gold, bonds and exchange,
Meeting the ocean's roar, beaten back by the sky,
    It creaks and rattles throughout a continent's range.

Honor is but a myth, integrity goes for naught.
    Wisdom is knowing how a man may gather the fruit
While his neighbor shakes the tree : the noblest use for thought,
    To know when talking is gain and when to be mute.

Doctors from colleges prate, clergymen talk against time,
    Big with oracular words, cunning with Hebraic lore,
Believing labor a curse, the penalty placed on crime,
    As the grand old Hierarchs held in the days of yore.

Better the hodden gray that is weft by a virtuous hand;

  Better the calm, still man who lives by the plow and spade;

Better the Sabine farm with its seven acres of land,

  Than streets that are built by the dirty channels of trade.

Wherein is a nation's wealth ? In what is a nation great ?

  Does a world-wide history prove that gold is the highest good ?

Could riches, and pomp, and show save Rome from her well

        earned fate ?

  Are the old time failures of nations understood ?

Did ever a people fail who only strove for the right,

  Who taught the nation's youth to be virtuous, brave and wise ?

Did ever a nation's sun sink down to a moral night,

  Till a nation's counsels were filled with the devil's lies ?

Once, when my soul was weary of wading in tangled thought,

  I slept by an attic window that looked to the bleak northeast.

And a dream came over my spirit, so clearly, vividly wrought,

  That it warned like the mystic hand at the Tyrant's feast.

THE DREAM.

    A week of scorching fever, when the hours

    Seemed stretched to days of torture, and the days

    Spun slowly out to months of groping pain.

    A sick man's oft told horrors: moping shapes

    That crawled and glared about with fishy eyes;

    Mouthing and threatening heads, that grew or shrank

From out the dusky corners of the room ;
Chattering tiresome forms of bird or ape
That perched themselves familiarly upon
The hideous posts which sentineled the bed,
Each post a mocking face.   And one came there
More dreadful than the rest ;— a sleepless fiend ;
Whose office was to crouch at the bed's foot,
And see to't, that no wink of sleep should cross
The burning eyelids or the hot, tired brain,
By night or day.   In vain they freely gave
The opiates that crazed but could not lull.
For, even as there came a drowsy sense
Of lessening pain, and the tired brow began
To reel and stagger toward forgetfulness,
Would rise that loathsome form with reptile eyes,
Mumming and mouthing at my white, scared face,
Till sleep was changed to deathless vigilance.

And so at last I came to understand
That 'twas my fate to die ; and that or rest,
Or sleep, for me on earth was none.   Ah God,
I do believe that he who has not felt
The rasping fire of fever in his veins,
When the hot blood becomes **as** molten lead,
And every nerve a lightning heated wire
To telegraph the pain in every part
Knows not what torture means.

There is a bound
Beyond whose limit pain is merged in death,
Most mercifully; — And, 'twill chance at times
That he who has his hand upon the latch
Which opens his own tomb, shall find himself
Gifted with such a wondrous speed of thought,
Such apprehension, and electric power
Of intuition, as the man in health
May never know or feel.   And thus it was,
That at the last I lay, helpless and mute,
Drawing with feeble care the failing breath,
That flickered doubtfully.   But with a mind
So clear, so active, quick to comprehend,
So strong in grasp and sudden to conceive,
That a whole life seemed mirrored in a thought.
Naught in the room escaped me as I lay,
Free from all pain, and conscious that my life
Hung by the merest thread.   The snuffy nurse,
Cat-footed, restless, moving to and fro,
As if impatient for the closing scene.
The sickening forces, standing in array
Of phial, pill and powder, with the dire
Medicinal chieftain — potent calomel.
The three wise men, for consultation met,
And holding conversation half aside,
Wisely debating on this drug or that;
Arguing if such and such might be

Allowed in dire extremity, and if
It could be proven from the books that Mott,
Or Abernethy had been known to give
Some certain tonic to a man, reduced
By fever to death's door.   And one who seemed
The leader of the trio, rose and stood,
With wooden face and spectacles on nose,
Beside the bed, and raised the thin white hand,
Placing a practised finger on the wrist,
Timing the scarce-felt pulses for, perchance,
Some two short minutes.   Then he turned away,
With something of the reverence and awe
That men will feel while standing by the dead,
And said, "the man is gone."

                    Ev'n as he spoke,
I smiled to think that one so learned and wise
Should err so simply in the question that
Affects our mortal breath   How could I die,
Yet lose no consciousness?   Where was the pang,
The mortal throe, the stoppage of the heart
And panting lungs ?   The fearful struggle which
Should wait on dissolution ?   None of these.
And yet the man was right.   The dying smile
Froze on the thin wan face ; the labored breath
Grew free, the weary senses fresh and strong.
The panting heart and brain awoke to life.

Buoyant and vigorous as when I climbed
Thy pine clad hills, O Mendon, in the flush
Of youth and health and hope, a joyous lad.
And this was death! This waking into life
With freshened strength and new born energy
Of soul; this casting off the earthly clog
That pains, and tires, and binds us to the earth.
Already the freed soul had turned and gazed
Half pityingly, half loathingly upon
Its wasted prison house of earthly clay,
Almost amused to see the snuffy nurse
Close ostentatiously the glazing eyes,
While weeping friends gathered about the bed,
Pitying the thin cold form that had become
But as the merest clod.

         And I became
Conscious of other forms within the room :
Old friends ; who had been freed long before
By this same dreaded death. Two radiant forms
Were these, that I had known in early youth,
When poverty and sickness pressed and clung
About them, till they rested in the earth,
Gladly, as doth a wearied infant seek
Its mother's breast. The one, an aged man,
A grandsire ; who on earth had drank the dregs
And lees of poverty ; but kept his faith

And stern integrity for eighty years,
Then sank into a nameless grave unknown,
But with God's noblest stamp upon his brow,—
An honest man.   And, as he yielded not
To dire temptation in his earthly needs,
So had he double honor in the land
Of disembodied souls.

                      And there was one
Whom I had known in childhood, and who might
Have blessed my later life, but that she passed
Beneath the bitter waters in her bloom
Of maiden loveliness, and was forgot
By all save him who loved her, and who kept
Her memory as a sacred thing apart.
These two, the maiden in her locks of gold
And aged grandsire, were as when on earth,
Inseparable; and 'twas theirs to see
That the freed soul, unused to roam in space,
Had proper guidance to the outer realms
Of the earth's influence, and be shown the way
Among the stars.

                 I would have lingered where
Old sympathies and recollections clung,
Sorrowing still awhile with those who mourned,
Of the earth, earthy.   But the radiant guides,

With sweet low voiccs, such as well might haunt
A poet lover in his dreams, said   " No :
Earth and earth's atmosphere are meet for man.
The soul, freed from its clay, may not abide
The rank, foul air, the sordid sins that grieve,
And bind, and slay.   The earth and all therein
Is giv'n to man.   We have no power to lift
A feather's weight from off his world of woe ;
Nor may we dwell for more than a brief space
Within his realm, where the foul air corrupts
With sickness, sin and death.   Come thou with us."

And we arose and passed away from earth
By the mere act of will, and with a speed
That set at naught the dull imperfect modes
Of earthly computation.   Naught to us
Was time, with its divisions and delays,
Nor any mode of reckoning by hours,
Or days, or years.   Being beyond the earth,
Alternate light and darkness were no more,
Nor day, nor night, nor the earth's atmosphere,
Nor any cloud nor shadow.   And I came
To know the golden mysteries that lie
Among the stars, in circumambient space.

There was a rapture in the new born life
That human language has no power to tell,—

A wealth of happiness and sweet content
That earth-bound souls may never understand.
The murky earth swung far away in space,
Hugged in a misty atmosphere, wherein
Were seething life, unceasing death, and all
Unwholesome things: and bearing on her face
The blotched and bloody record of her crimes,
We saw her reel on her allotted round,
Dimly and distantly, and only said,
Who in this better life would be so mad
As yield one year's existence in the skies
To have the fee in simple of yon world,
With all her land and gold, her petty strifes,
Her crimes and sins, with suffering interwrought—

      *   *   *   *   *

I woke.   The northeast wind beat at the pane,
   The village clock the hour of midnight tolled.
I heard the patter of the winter rain,
   And felt the chillness of the damp and cold.

Ah God, how mean appeared my dwelling place
   On earth ; how small and poor all earthly things.
I felt the poverty and deep disgrace
   That pauper princes feel, or throneless kings.

I said, 'Twas but a dream : and strove to keep
    A living interest in the life affairs
Of busy men, who work, and eat, and sleep
    Beneath a weary load of petty cares.

In vain.   All that had power to please before,
    Had lost the power of pleasing.   I was one
Fated to love his fellows nevermore,
    Nor join the headlong, greedy race they run.

I saw the emmets on this ragged earth
    Each struggling for his grain of yellow sand ;
I heard the hollow lie, and saw the dearth
    Of justice, truth, and honor in the land.

How could I mingle in the selfish throng
    That grasped and struggled, bit, and stung, and lied.
I, who had heard the morning stars in song,—
    What needs were mine that this had satisfied ?

And so we fell apart—the world and I.
    " A half mad poet "—so their prattle ran.
" One who cares not to thrive, or sell, or buy,
    And has small liking for his fellow man.

" He had a fever once ; and in a dream,
    Went far beyond the limits of this earth ;
At least he says so.   And since then 'twould seem,
    Cares naught for money or for money's worth."

And so I came at last, by slow degrees,
  To shun the meeting of a human face,
To seek the beetling crag where gnarly trees,
  Root-anchored in the rock, have dwelling place.

Losing desire for human speech, I found
  A runic language in the song of birds.
I learned to understand each woodland sound,—
  The sybil trees and all their mystic words.

I dwelt with nature in her solitudes,
  And learned to love her in her wildest dress.
A mother to me in her milder moods,
  And in her savage moments scarcely less.

I climbed the mountain when the early dew
  Glistened on balm-flowers where the wild bee hummed.
For me the woodcook whirred; the goshawk flew
  Low o'er the thicket where the partridge drummed.

The round-topped pines sighed far beneath my feet,
  The mountain stream shone through the morning mist.
I watched the valley where bright waters meet
  From icy springs the sun has never kissed.

Cleaving the pool the gleaming fish-hawk shot,
  With aim unerring on his finny prey.
The wild-cat stole from briar sheltered grot,
  The pert kingfisher chattered from his spray.

I loved the deep, dark forest, where no foot
　Of all-polluting man had left a trace.
I loved the pine tree with its rock-bound root,
　And low, sweet whispers of a holier place.

And thus, half hermit and half misanthrope,
　I dragged the listless years of a decade.
Dreamily musing, without wish or hope,
　Watching the seasons blossom, fill and fade.

Men called me Infidel — God save the mark —
　For that I went not in their fanes to hear
A blind man rustling parchment in the dark,
　A creed-clock ticking on the drowsy ear.

GLEANING AFTER THE FIRE.

WE tread a weary and blackened plain,
　　Missing the good that we most desire,
Our way is soddened by mist and rain
　　That follows the track of blasting fire.
We falter and pause, as one who gropes
　　For a way more pleasant and something higher,
Passing the graves of our buried hopes,
　　Like him who gleans on the track of fire.

We strain each muscle, and sob and choke,
　　To gain a march on the desolate scene ;
For we see, through rifts of the blinding smoke
　　Bright gleams of flowers and banks of green.
We know the singing of birds is there,
　　And murmur of brooks we may not hear.
We know that the land is fresh and fair,
　　And the way we travel is dead and sere.

At times we trust we are gaining ground,
　　But the murky line of the fire recedes.
Our ears catch only the hollow sound
　　Of baseless dogmas and jarring creeds.

When strength was failing we paused to ask
  Is there nothing better, and is this all?
Is life-long labor a bootless task
  To end at last in a dead blank wall?

Is the struggle of self the highest aim?
  Is naught to be gained by noble deeds?
From the crackling stubble the answer came
  In a babel of tongues and jarring creeds.
We passed the bones of the martyred dead
  Who perished by rack, and cord, and flame;
And shrank from the lying priest who said
  That Christ and the Twelve would do the same.

And ever the priest was at our side,
  And ever he threatened and lied and fawned.
And ever proclaimed himself a guide
  Through the murky fire to the fields beyond,
But our hearts are deadened to priestly ire,
  Our ears are deaf to the priestly call;
We glean in silence behind the fire,
  And look for rest at the dead, blank wall.

LINES FOR THE TIMES.

HO ! fellow workmen, one and all,
 In mill and mine, or lanes of traffic,
Behold the Hand upon the wall!
The mystic writing, terse and graphic.
 The priceless heritage we hold
Slips through our hands to foes and strangers,
 While Honor trades for place or gold,
And Freedom kneels to money changers.

The stern, true way the Fathers taught
 Has passed away with those who taught it.
The honor they so dearly bought
 Rests in the grave, with those who bought it.
We retrograde thro' each decade,
 The statesman sinks to politician.
We mark with sordid lines of trade
 The caste of plebeian or patrician.

We teach the nation's youth to wade
 In moral filth of sharp finessing;
That Godliness is thrifty trade,
 And sudden wealth the chiefest blessing.

The trickster and the shameless guile,
  With brazen frauds and lying faces,
Disgrace the nation's forum; while
  Corruption rules in highest places.

Alas, there is no God but gold;
  No good, save riches or position.
Our chosen ones are bought and sold,
  Their names sink down to swift perdition.
They laugh the pilgrim sires to scorn ;
  On every sea their ships are sailing.
So that they win the oil and corn,
  What though the grand old cause be failing ?

The gifts that time has held in store ;
  The wisdom governed by the sages;
The treasured wealth of ancient lore,
  We hold in trust for future ages.
The gifts are laid before our eyes,
  The riches wait for us to use them.
To take, if we be strong and wise,
  If weak and trifling, to refuse them.

If we, whose sinews pay for all,
  Through weak defense, ill-timed and aimless,
Allow our cause to go in thrall
  Shall coming ages hold us blameless?

We have the lesson taught by Rome,

    The more our shame that we should need it.

The application lies at home —

    The better for us if we heed it.

What if the garnered wealth and lore

    Be dowered on souls that shun and flee them?

Or godlike gems and diadems

    Be held to eyes that will not see them?

We have the right: we have the might:

    The rhyme is meet for the occasion.

Who seeks the light shall see the light —

    Who shuns it woos his own damnation.

DRAWERS AND HEWERS.

BY A HEWER.

WE stand where our great-great-grandsires stood,
   Working in silence—ashamed to sing.
The ax sinks deep in the frozen wood,
   The buckets go to the icy spring;
We work and listen in sullen mood,
   As over the valley the axes ring—
Drawers of water—Hewers of wood.

Drawers of water, Hewers of wood :
   We know the story—'tis very old.
And something better 'tis understood,
   Than when we molded the calf of gold
Which Moses and Aaron turned to the good
   Of God—knows who : we are always sold,
We, Drawers of water and Hewers of wood.

We hewed for the temple of Solomon,
   We drew for the rulers of all the east,
We hewed for the mighty Babylon.

For thousands of years we have never ceased
To hew or draw when the fit was on
    For palace or church with king or priest—
Then sat at the gate till the feast was done.

The heavier work the lighter pay :
    Such is the rule the wide world o'er.
For the idler, a constant holiday.
    " To him that hath shall be given more :
From him that not ye shall take away
    The little he hath."   Oh blessed lore !
Is there anything left for us to say ?

They take the corn that they do not reap
    And leave us only the coarsest fare,
With the straw, perchance, whereon to sleep ;
    'Tis theirs the Tyrian robes to wear.
They make the laws that they do not keep,—
    Then offer to God a formal prayer,
And strangle His image for stealing sheep.

And all of the Good we hold to-day
    Has cost us ages of toil to wring
From Hebrew letter, from usage gray,
    And the harpy clutches of priest and king.
We work and wait for the better way
    The snail-paced ages are sure to bring,—
But we grind the bayonets while we pray.

Drawers and hewers, we watch and wait,
  For the brighter dawning shall come at last.
We shall find the key of the golden gate,
  And take a bond for the bitter past.
And kings and prelates shall yield to fate
  When none of us pay, or pray, or fast,
For the harlot wedding of Church and State.

Drawers and Hewers! be ours the blame,
  If the coming ages shall still rehearse
The bloody drama with bootless aim,
  Or the coward cringing to place and purse.
Lock hands for the right!   The priestly game
  Shall fail, when a wakened universe
Dare call the wrong by its Saxon name.

THE SMITHS.

LET us say that the lives of our sires are lost;
   That the siren, hope, will elude and fade;
That the ages are blackened and battle tossed,
  And we gain no step in a long decade.
What then, shall the wrong and the crime exhaust
  Eternal justice? And shall no shade
Remain of the life that is crushed and crossed?

Let us say we have gained so much on time
  That we hold some good which their lives have bought;
That not in vain at the wrong and crime
  Have Freedom's battles been aimed and fought;
That even failure may be sublime
  In its fearful cost, in the lesson taught,
And its deathless lay in the realms of rhyme.

Alas for the Workers who cringe, or shun
  The work cut out for their hands to do!
Alas for the poets who praise and pun!

Alas for the Triflers the wide world through,
And the manly race that is seldom run,
  The wise contempt for the just and true,
The much to do and the little done!

And oh, for an unbought pen to brand
  The sordid tricks of these latter days ;
And a harp too nobly true and grand
  To hymn a patron's or prince's praise—
One that shall sweep with an Odic hand
  The carpet bards with their tomtit lays,
As the wild Missouri sweeps the sand.

DISHEARTENED.

IN cottage, palace, saloon or street,
  We meet with a friendly nod or smile;
  And little we know the weary while
Of the sick and withering hearts we meet.

We carry a mask to hide a woe;
  We drag a burden from place to place;
  And no one sees, through a smiling face,
That a soul sits wringing her hands below.

We hide our burdens as best we may,
  We potter and palter to present things;
  We kneel at the thrones of money kings,
And pawn our manhood, and pass away

To be forgotten.   'Tis just as well.
  We pool our lives with the struggling crowd.
  We listen to voices, blatant, loud,
Of Rights and Wrongs, and Heaven or Hell,

And say to.ourselves, no mortal knows
    The whence we came or whither we go,
    Or whether one creed be true or no,
Or aught that governs our last repose.

I sit and listen, and think, and wait:
    I rise at five in the wintry murk
    To ponder and delve at weary work,
And look in vain for the golden gate.

My failing eyes shall never behold
    But dead, white hills in the morning gray,
    And cold, dull gleams at the close of day,
And gates beyond — that are not of gold.

TO JOHN BULL—ON HIS CHRISTMAS.

IT'S little I care for a holiday,
    And less for a lord or peer,
But I have a simple word to say
In a workman's rough, untutored way,
    On the opening of the year.

I know the poets will clink their rhymes,
    As they always have done before,
And ring the changes of Christmas chimes,
On beef, and pudding, and good old times,
    As they did in the days of yore.

But thousands of paupers will shrink and pine,
    As they list to the Christmas song,
And sneer at your charities thin and fine,
Drawn and leveled by rule and line,
    As they hunger, and wait, and long.

For your Christmas mirth is a make-believe
    That covers a cancerous sore.
And you know that millions must fast and grieve,
That mothers and children must starve or thieve;
    But you choose to gloze it o'er.

Then sing your carol and play your play,
  For why should you pity or feel?
If a starving wretch should call to-day,
Bribe his misery out of your way —
  Give him for once a meal.

Only for once — and the workhouse then:
  'Tis the best the fellow can do.
He's but a thriftless pauper; and when
He has lost all caste with his fellow men
  Pray why should he bother you?

Respectable John, with your shaven face,
  Are you up to their priestly tricks?
You'd break your legs to speak with "his Grace" —
Have you ever revolved a nation's case,
  Whose paupers are one in six?

A Bishop with seventy thousand pounds,
  Filched each year from the workman's pay.—
Do you wonder, when on your treadmill rounds
With the fools who shout for miters and crowns,
  If there isn't a better way?

OUR LITTLE PRINCE.

"LITTLE CHARLEY is a prince,"
   So we said in joyous pride,
As we loitered side by side,
Where the roses bloomed and died,
Half a dozen summers since.

He was rustling through the leaves,
   Where the golden tassels swayed,
   Half in pleasure, half afraid,
   Hiding in the furrowed shade,
Where the August cricket grieves.

Silken tassels on the corn,
   Silken curls about his head;
   "Which is which?" we laughing said;
   While the sun a glory shed
On the curls and tasseled corn.

Saxon eyes and face and hair,
  Saxon blood in every vein,
  Cheeks like roses after rain;
  Never shall we see again
Childish loveliness so rare.

When the apple and the quince
  All their summer fragrance shed,
  How we miss our darling dead;
  How we miss the curly head
Of our lovely little prince.

Little Charley *was* a prince—
  But, somebody in the sky
  Had more need of him than I,
  So we laid him down to die
Half a dozen summers since.

IT DOES NOT PAY.

Inscribed to the memory of " Uncle John Mayo," a Puritan freethinker, *sans peur et sans reproche.*   If my lines were as good as the man, I could discount Milton.

A BENT old man with silvery hair,
    A palsied hand and brow of care,
  Sat in the shade on a summer day.
And he musingly said with thoughtful air,
      It does not pay.

For years he had mixed in the world's turmoil
Of busy strife, and with manly toil
  Had battled many a weary day.
And ever the world was still his foil.
      It did not pay.

Partners had swindled and friends betrayed,
Those he had succored refused their aid
  When adverse storms rose over the way.
He only said as he sat in the shade,
      It does not pay.

No bitterness lurked in the old man's heart,
Bravely and well he had played his part
   In the game of life, and well might say,
As he backward looked on the troubled chart,
      It does not pay.

Restfully, peacefully sat he there ;
The south wind lifted his thin white hair
   As it lightly blew in tender play.
He only said with a patient air,
      It does not pay.

Eighty summers their blossoms had shed,
Eighty winters had whitened his head,
   He waited his summons day by day ;
Life is a feverish dream, he said,
      It does not pay.

THE HUNTER'S LAMENT.

MY boy is dead, my pet, my own.
   The crescent moon, with silver light,
  Gleams on his lowly grave. To-night,
I take the trail of life alone.

Four years ago, I fondly said,
  Lo, unto me a son is born.
  And when the west wind waked the morn
The mother of my boy was dead.

I have no joy in heaven's light,
  I can not weep and will not pray.
  I wear the dreary night to day,
I tire the weary day to night.

With dark surplice and oily voice
  Comes one who speaks to me of peace.
  "The boy has gone where sorrows cease,
'Twere meet the father should rejoice."

My soul in fierceness makes reply :
My beautiful, my dark-eyed boy,
Whose very being was a joy,
What had he done that he should die !

Over the somber hill of pines
The night-wind sweeps with chastened wail,
Shaking against the moonbeams pale
The tangled hair of untrained vines.

The fox barks sharply from the hill
As fades the light adown the west.
Soothing his mate upon her nest,
Plaintively mourns the whip-poor-will.

Out from the shadows weird and grim
Where fitful gleams of moonlight fall,
I hear the owlet's hollow call
Ring through the forest arches dim.

The dun deer feed at early morn
Where lilies nod by purling brooks :
Still hangs the rifle on its hooks,
Still am I restless and forlorn.

My rifle rusts against the wall,
My hound tugs idly at his chain,

I care not for the summer rain,
Or if the golden apples fall.

I know 'tis weakness thus to moan—
    That men should suffer and be strong,
    But oh, the journey seems so long!
And 'tis so sad to be alone!

Why should I o'er the mountain toil?
    Where is the pleasure, what the need
· To draw with skill the deadly bead
When none are left to share the spoil?

My home is desolate.   Nor wife,
    Nor joyous child will greet me more.
    What wonder that I ponder o'er
My grief, or weary of my life?

IDA MAY.

IT is twenty years ago, Ida May. It is twenty years ago
      That we sat beneath the moon
      In the pleasant month of June,
In the shadow of a hawthorn white as snow, Ida May.

'Twas a pleasant, foolish time, Ida May. 'Twas a pleasant, fool-
   ish time,
      Watching thus the golden gleam
      Of the moonlight on the stream,
While we listened to the pleasant village chime, Ida May.

We are older now than then, Ida May. We are older now
   than then,
      And have wisdom, it may be.
      But the happy hearts, and free,
Blithesome laughter we can never feel again, Ida May.

Time will run us down at last, Ida May. Time will run us
   down at last.
      I've a slight rheumatic twinge,
      And your tresses have the tinge
Of a color you'll be apt to find is fast, Ida May. Of a color
   you'll be apt to find is fast.

IONE.

'TIS a word of rhythmic measure, is that dulcet name, Ione,
Borrowed from the maids of Athens, meaning aged, or
alone.
Can the meaning be prophetic, O my blue-eyed one, my own?

Do you wander by the waters when the sun is warm in May
With young hopes as freshly springing as they did upon a day
Some few years before this writing—six or seven, let us say?

Have you found the world grow colder, have you learned that
hopes will fade,
That the winters are more bitter, and more frail the summer
shade?
And that nothing is so certain as the fellow with the spade?

For I knew you were ambitious half a dozen years ago;
That you longed for rank and riches. But I also chanced to
know
That a **loving** heart was pulsing in the quiet depths below.

So I watched you like a lover as you jostled in the tide
Of those selfish social wrestlers, with no helper at your side,
And I thought that you might triumph, just by dint of pluck
and pride.

But the strife has been a hard one—you are just a little pale—
'Twould. have been so grand to triumph ; it is no disgrace to fail,
For the odds were high against you, and you were so weak and
    frail.

Ah, the springs are wet and heavy, and the summers dull and
    tame.
Black and windy are the autumns—every day shall bear its blame,
But it is not in the seasons—'tis that we are not the same.

Sitting in the grand old forest, listening idly, all alone,
To the gentle pattering raindrops and the pine-tree's monotone,
Is it wonder that my musing turned upon thee, sweet Ione ?

Our two lives have naught in common, and our paths must
    still diverge ;
Yours on quiet inland waters, mine upon the outer surge—
Yours to trill a summer sonnet, mine to chant a winter dirge.

When old age shall find us wanting all the joys we hoped to win,
Striving idly in our weakness with the bitter thoughts within,
Shall we think of sweet Maud Muller, and the things that
    might have been ?

ALL THINGS COME ROUND.

" All things come round to him who will but wait."—*Tales of a Wayside Inn.*

"ALL things come round to him who will but wait."
    Ah poet ! were thy rhythmic words but true,
We said, and closed the book.   For our estate
    Was at its lowest ebb ; and heavy grew
The bitter "income tax laid on by fate,"
    Which is evaded by the lucky few,
And is assessed in such a pleasant way,
That, all the less you have, the more you pay.

"All things come round."   Much, much has come to us,
    That we had been well satisfied to miss.
The tolling bell, slow creaking in its rust ;
    The trusted lips, that sold us with a kiss ;
The coffins, that were lowered into dust ;
    The griefs we might not tell ; the serpent hiss
Of slander ; loss of health or worldly gear,
And hopes, that turned up blanks from year to year.

'Tis sad to find how little that is worth
    For which we waited long.   'Tis sadder still
To find the hearts we trusted most on earth—
    Not dead—but dull, indifferent, and chill.
'Tis sad to see the roof above the hearth
    We loved in childhood, at a stranger's will
Torn down for some new whim of innovation
In gewgaw taste, or modern speculation.

But sadder far than this, than these, than all,
    Is loss of youth—the Mayday of the soul.
To see the years close round us like a pall,
    To feel our lives unrolling a blank scroll :
The head becoming like a billiard ball,
    Eyes failing, teeth decaying, and the whole
Anatomy gone into liquidation,
To close a very pressing obligation.

MY WOODLAND PRINCESS.

WHAT if we met in an old log-road
    Where the leaf-mold clung to her small bare heels,
  And instead of woodland flowers, her load
Was a string of trout and silver eels?

Her gown was ragged and limp with dew,
    But it rounded a pàir of splendid hips.
A rich red torrent was flashing through
    Her startled pulses to cheeks and lips.

The wholesome bronze of her ruddy face
    Was like ripe fruit in a bower of green,
And she walked the wold with the easy grace
    And firm, free step of a woodland queen.

The dew had moistened the jetty hair
    That waved and clustered about her head.
I caught a glimpse of the shoulders bare,
    The sparkling eyes and the lips of red.

Only a glimpse of the tattered gown,
    As she disappeared in the leafy way.
A glance of the shoulders plump and brown,
    And a face—that haunted me night and day.

And I wandered on by the yeasty stream
  To try for the trout that would not rise,
For I walked all day in a misty dream
  Of lips, and shoulders, and curls and eyes.

And I thought of a damsel, city bred,
  Of narrow shoulders and doubtful spine,
With false hair frizzed on the trifling head,
  And false life, beveled by rule and line.

Unskilled, unheeding in wifely cares,
  Expensive, vapory, worthless : when
The mother half hates the child she bears,
  Where shall we go for the nation's men ?

I take the lot that the fates decree,
  And my fancies fail me, one by one,
But often in dreams again I see
  The Woodland Princess of Cedar Run.

REMEMBERED—L. K.

LONG years ago, in early June,
When brooks and birds were in high tune,
I sat beneath an oak at noon,—

A grand old oak of grateful shade;
And at my side a dark·eyed maid
Who listened, and was not afraid.

Her eyes were moist with pearly tears;
She whispered that in later years
We would divide our hopes and fears.

For years, long years, it was my dream,
An idle *ignis fatuus* gleam
Of moonlight on a frozen stream.

 * * * * * *

I passed that way when years had fled,
I could not find the streamlet's bed,
The oak was withered, sere and dead.

Oft, as I brush my locks of gray,
I muse upon that summer day;
The shady oak, and streamlet's play.

MOTHER AND CHILD.

Mrs. E. Vanatter committed suicide by drowning in the summer of 1856. She took her little boy along.

DIMLY the light of a summer morn
   Shadowed the willow and white hawthorn.
Far in the east pale streaks of gray
Faintly tokened the coming day.

In the morning dim, thro' the rank wet grass,
A woman's form did wearily pass —
Passed, with uncertain step and slow,
To the banks of a stream that slept below.

And ever with loving tones she wiled,
As she held by the hand her only child,
Who upward gazed with a strange surprise
At the gleaming light of her sad dark eyes.

"I was sleeping warm in my little bed,
And why did you bring me here?" he said.

"The world is bitter, my darling child,"
She said, and her eye grew strangely wild,
"Bitter and cold; and we are lone.
Wilt go with thy mother, my loved, my own?"

Oh a strange, sad sight was that mother pale,
Whispering gently a fairy tale,
A sweet wild tale of a beautiful home
Fathoms beneath the snowy foam.

And the boy grew calm, and sank to rest
In child-like faith, on his mother's breast.
Sank to rest on the grassy shore
That his little feet shall press no more.

The sun has silvered a thousand rills,
Warmed the valleys and brightened the hills,
Casting aslant a golden beam
Where sleeps the mother beneath the stream.
Calmly sleeps in a dreamless rest,
With the boy she loved on her gentle breast.

The white hawthorn has scattered its flowers
To the summer winds in fragrant showers.
The willow trees on the streamlet's verge
Are softly singing a sweet, low dirge;
A requiem sad, a mourning lay,
With whispering voice that seems to say,
Passing away — passing away.

BESSIE IRELAN.

BESSIE IRELAN was a queen,
    Regal brow and dusky hair,
  Deep blue eyes and queenly air,
  Good and kind as she was fair—
Sweeter maid was never seen.

Bessie Irelan was a queen
    All who knew her freely owned;
    But the crown was only loaned.
    Bessie Irelan was dethroned
On the turn of seventeen.

I am older now than when
    To her crown I bent the knee,
    And it drove me wild to see
    How she queened it over me,
How she ruled the hearts of men.

It is twenty years to-day
    Since she gave her crown in trust
    To a sordid soul of rust,
    One who trailed it in the dust
Ere the year had passed away.

'Twere a better fate by half
　　That the village bell had tolled
　　For the maiden pale and cold,
　　Than to be with links of gold
Chained to such a golden calf.

Soul of poesy and fire,
　　Dreeing weary years of pain,
　　Galled and wounded by the chain—
　　Have they dragged her all in vain
Through their sordid lanes of mire?

Yesterday, the village bell
　　By the ancient sexton rung,
　　Counted with its iron tongue
　　Thirty-seven, as it swung,
Slowly creaking to her knell.

And to-day they take her where
　　She will never see the sun.
　　Now her earthly race is done
　　Has a better life begun?
Shall I ever know her there?

A LITTLE GRAVE.

I SIT by the window with Maud, my wife,
　　Watching the drift of the wind and rain;
The tree-tops writhing like things of life,
　　And the sweep of the storm across the plain.

We strive to be merry. — O dull deceit
　　That cannot deceive; for well we know
That the mutual smile is a mutual cheat—
　　Our hearts are out in the soddened snow.

Out, where the arms of the oaks are tossed,
　　And a white stone faces the bitter west.
Where two little childish hands are crossed
　　In the cold wet clay, on a baby breast.

And it seems such a heartless thing to sit
　　In a cozy room, so pleasant and warm,
Watching the wraith-like shadows flit
　　O'er the little grave, in the driving storm.

We turn from the window, and strive to smile,
   But the false light fades from the brimming eyes.
We strive for a subject that may beguile,
   And our two white faces are two white lies.

      .

Late, late in the night, when the silken curls
   Are veiling an arm where the bright head rests,
I can feel the warmth of the dewy pearls,
   And the weary rise of the snowy breast.

And once in a way a man may weep
   At the mother sorrow that slumbers there,
As she murmurs a something in her sleep,
   That is half a cradle-song, half a prayer.

A SUMMER NIGHT.

WEST sloping hills smile to the setting sun
    In richest summer hues of vivid green.
The mower whistles, as, his labor done,
   He homeward takes his way. In distance seen,
Like wreaths of smoke along the meadow's edge,
The white fog marks the river's banks of sedge.

The distant cattle, lowing loud and clear,
    Are wending homeward, leisurely and slow.
The farm dog's bark comes softened to the ear
    By mellowing distance. On the stream below,
With ever ready wing and watchful eye
A flock of wild-fowl gracefully glide by.

The hermit thrush sings from the topmost spray
    Of fir or hemlock; from the thicket dense
The gray owl hoarsely calls. A plaintive lay
    Is rising from the ivy clustered fence
That skirts the base of yonder wooded hill —
An eager, flute-like call of whip-poor-will.

The plover's cry cuts sharply on the air,
    The clumsy beetle blunders on his rounds;
The wary fox creeps softly from his lair
    And barks defiance to the distant hounds,
Who answer back with fierce, defiant bay,
And tug their chains, and pant to be away.

Now swims the moon along the milky way
    In burnished splendor; and the hours of night
March forth like conquerors who hold mild sway,
    Dispensing golden dreams, and rest, and light,
Alike on cottage, hut, or princely hall,
A peaceful benison, dowered alike on all.

WRECK OF THE GLOUCESTER.

The ship Gloucester sank in sight of land near Boston harbor, some ninety years ago. A young merchant, whose name I have forgotten, had a wife and brother on board, and was also part owner of the ship and cargo. He saw the Gloucester from South Boston heights, when she foundered, in a furious gale. From that time until his death he was a mild maniac, watching the sea and wandering up and down the beach, especially in rough weather. He lived to the age of eighty.

THE shrieking winds are up and away,
And a bent old man with locks of gray
Watches the clouds through the blinding spray.

For fifty years, when the winds were high,
He has walked the sands and watched the sky,
With maundering step and restless eye.

Crooning and muttering o'er and o'er
The tale of a ship that sailed from shore,
And returned to port—ah, nevermore!

A noble ship. And centered there
Was all that he held most dear and fair.
She sank; and his life was a blank despair.

It is fifty years since he heard the toll
Of the good ship's bell, and over his soul
The waters swept with a heavy roll.

Wandering vacantly to and fro,
Watching the ships that come and go,
And the white crowned waters ebb and flow.

Out in the offing, side by side,
Bride and brother, brother and bride,
They rise and sink with the sobbing tide.

HASTE.

THE rapid strides of this latter age
 Bring all our tardy plans to grief,
  And fortune has learned to turn the leaf
Before we have time to read the page.

A CHRISTMAS ENTRY.

BY AN IRON MERCHANT.

SHALL I sing a song on the bleak new year,
    When the snow lies deep on valley and plain —
Shall I chirp of winter and Christmas cheer,
    Or pipe to the season a gay refrain?

I will sing of a maiden I knew of old,
    Ere my heart was chilled or my head was gray —
Of a Saxon maiden, with locks of gold,
    Who walked with me in the vanished way.

For the skies are gloomier ever since
    They took her off on the loathsome bier;
And a deadness broods on the autumn tints,
    And a vapid taste on the Christmas cheer.

So, Nancy Shepard, I sing of you,
    In the Dorian strain of early days.
I will praise your eyes of the deepest blue,
    Your winsome looks and your winning ways.

For you were fairest where all were fair;
  Where all were graceful you were the Grace.
You walked the world with a queenly air,
  And the light of heaven was in your face.

Alas for the life you were meant to bless;
  Alas for the riches that rot and rust;
Alas, that beauty and loveliness
  Should fade so soon to the common dust.

And I, who have turned my fiftieth year,
  Watching the coming and going ships,
Am entering items of beauty here,
  To eyes of azure and coral lips!

A hard-faced merchant, in love with gain,
  Wise in the ways of the Rascal Man—
Shall I change my white winged birds o' the main
  For a lovelorn ditty, and pipes, and Pan?

But I file away, as a thing apart,
  The cherished memory of that maid
In the warmest niche of a world-worn heart.
  The rest may go—to the winds of trade.

For the world is cunning, and hard, and cold;
  And the life we live has so little in't;—
Like a walking body without a soul—
  Or a julep—without the ice and mint.

TWO LIVES.

THEY sat with their small white feet in the brook—
 Two village maidens of beauty rare.
Kate, with her bright *espiegle* look,
 And blue-eyed Blanche in her golden hair.

They bathed the ankles so trim and neat,
 They laved the breasts and the round white arms,
They plashed the water with dainty feet,
 And laughed and glowed in their maiden charms.

The air was fragrant with new-mown hay,
 The wild bee wrought with drowsy hum ,
And they chatted the dreamy hours away
 With girlish plans for the years to come.

And she with the eyes of sparkling jet,
 Would be content as a farmer's wife ;
To shun the follies that wear and fret
 In the simple pleasures of country life.

Then Blanche, with her laughing eyes of blue,
 Shook down a river of sunny hair
That rippled and flowed in golden hue,
 O'er neck, and bosom, and shoulders bare.

"And I," she said, "would live in the town,
  With lackeys to go or come at call.
And I should be proud, if men would crown
  Me queen of beauty, at rout or ball."

Oh, Blanche, in your veil of golden hair,
  No sybil you, of the future life.
On you, in your beauty ripe and rare,
  Shall fall the lot of the farmer's wife.

And your soul will tire of the petty gains,
  And the work-day trifles that wear the time,
And matron worry and mother-pains
  Shall waste your beauty before its prime.

And red-lipped Kate, with her midnight curls,
  Shall win the riches for which you pine,
Her brow shall glisten with gems and pearls,
  Her board shall sparkle with plate and wine.

But she will long for the new-mown hay,
  And the gusty shadows on upland leas ;
And sicken and tire of her splendid way,
  And sigh for the brooks, and birds, and bees.

And you shall chafe at your narrow lot,
  And weary and tire of your household cares.
And each shall covet what each has not,
  And pine for the burden the other bears.

Oh, city dame, and oh, farmer's wife,
　Too much forgetting—too long estranged,
Ye were two jewels of love and life—
　If but the setting were turned or changed.

———

ELAINE.

ELAINE, my bright-eyed, my sunlight, my passion,
　Lay your proud head on my bosom to-night.
Old loves and old love-songs have gone out of fashion,
　And Mammon is king, by divinest of right.

Press the full breasts that are lovingly beating,
　Close to the heart that is throbbing for you.
Shut out the moonlight. The night is too fleeting.—
　Oh, lips that are moist with the soul's honey-dew,
Draw hard on the spirit through lips that, responding,
　As powder to fire, flash their blood-life to you.

Press **me**, oh press me, strong-handed, white-throated,
　To your rosy-tipped bosom, till daylight peeps through
The casement, o'er landscapes starlighted, moss-moated,
　And the tame upland meadows thick jeweled with dew.

ANNA FAY—ON SKATES.

TO RAB.

SHE glanced and gleamed from place to place
On curving lines of easy grace,
And such a form—and such a face!

Cutting her name with scroll and curve,
We watched her sway and sweep and swerve—
Elastic health in every nerve.

Each cheek was just a damask rose,
Her mouth, a bud that did unclose
O'er beads of pearl in two white rows.

Her little feet glanced here and there ;
She tossed her bonnet—anywhere,
And gave the winds her wealth of hair.

The night breeze kissed her chestnut curls
As round she flew in dizzy whorls—
The very queen of village girls.

Fair maids are not so scarce ; and they
Were out that night upon the Bay,
But none so fair as Anna Fay.

                    *

And Billy Jones, fastidious Bill,
Who owned the mansion on the hill,
And did—whatever pleased his will ;

Cute Bill, who never got done brown ;
Who dealt in farms the country round,
And stores, and corner lots in town ;

Shrewd Bill—our village millionaire,
Who drove his crabs with such an air—
What business had *he* skating there ?

Unlucky Bill ! woe worth the day
That pretty witch, sweet Anna Fay,
Skated your foolish heart away.

            *   *

Eight years have passed.   The mansion still
Looks from the summit of the hill,
Where, like a lord, reigned bachelor Bill.

Ah, Mrs. Jones, I needs must say,
You wield a most despotic sway ;
I liked you more as Anna Fay.

Moral.

Now, bachelors who read this sonnet,
   Be well admonished while you may,
   Don't be enticed nor led astray
By any she that wears a bonnet.
   There's many a lovely nymph to-day
   As sharp—on skates—as Anna Fay.
Keep off the ice when they are on it!

PARAPHRASE ON " BRAHMA."

THE slayer but obeys the Fates,
  A better change awaits the slain,
All things my essence permeates,
  As the parched earth the summer rain.

The same, a thousand years ago, to-day;
  To-day, a thousand ages hence.
Can time, or fame, or shame outgrow
  Omniscience or omnipotence?

I fly with him who flies from me;
  He faints, in me he finds his rest;
He doubts; from doubt I set him free.
  All doubt is buried in my breast.

All things are mine, and mine all needs,
  And mine the fogs of mysticism—
The chrismal vail of heathen creeds,
  The senseless myths of Brahminism.

THE RETIRED PREACHER.

A MAN he was of most benignant mien,
   Of portly size and countenance serene,
Who, though his flowing beard and locks were hoar,
Used no disgusting mixtures to restore.
Of genteel habits, cleanly to a fault,
Using no liquors, spirituous or malt.
Ruddy of cheek, and straight in back and limb,
No gout or rheumatism affected him.
Temperate in habit, frugal in his ways,
His life serenely ran to length of days.
Well versed in all the topics of the time,
A judge of prose and lover of good rhyme ;
A writer too he was, of middling verse,
Of which full much he wrote, and often did rehearse.

Called early to the pulpit, nothing loth,
He pounded and expounded on the cloth
For three decades, in such a style and tone
He pleased the many while he angered none.
His little parish liked the young divine,
Whose voice was pleasant, and appearance fine.
He preached straightforwardly, in language plain,
And in good taste ; nor did he preach in vain.

To him came offerings from the nests of hens,

Fat turkeys and young capons from their pens.

For him the holidays brought scented notes,

With gifts of slippers, dressing gowns and coats.

And, being well housed, with much to eat and wear,

He found his master's cross an easy load to bear.

Always a fav'rite with the sisterhood,

Who found him *so* benevolent and good,

He knew the value of the softest place,

And dropped into it with a native grace.

Preaching forgiveness and the law of love,

He laid, no doubt, much treasure up above ;

But, feeling earthly needs, 'tis also clear

He managed to lay by some treasure here,

Keeping himself quite harmless to the eyes

Of worldly people, he was also wise.

Pleasing, for he had studied how to please,

He passed the quiet days in virtuous ease,

While, spinning not, and liking ill to toil,

He still absorbed his share of carnal corn and oil.

Thus, walking pleasantly life's fitful stage,

Good Doctor Mickle reached a green old age.

At sixty years, sedate, reserved and wise,

Full many sought the Doctor's sage advice,

Accorded freely unto all who sought,

But most benignly to the ones who brought

Fresh girlish faces, with bright eyes and curls—
For he excelled in counseling young girls ;
Giving much time to maiden protegés
In moonlight walks, beneath the village trees ;
Leading the ductile mind in paths of peace,
Such as were taught in academic Greece,
Taking, no doubt, a mild platonic pride
In walking wisdom's paths,—with Venus at his side.

Envious detraction, rife on every hand,
Admitted that the Doctor's ways were bland,
His presence fine, with excellent physique.
Also, he knew sŏme Latin and less Greek,
With just how far a Latin phrase should go,
And when 'twere wise to know—or not to know.
But his fine head, white with the frost of years,
Was all too heavy just behind the ears.
His piety, mixed with shrewd worldly sense,
The envious claimed as cunning and pretence.
And business men, of sharp, successful lives,
Eschewed his protegés when seeking wives,
Thinking the Doctor's pleasant ways no less
Than private paths, well trodden to his own success.

And I ? Well, I have naught to say,
    Being outside of church dominion.
I let things wag the natural way
    And leave each man his own opinion.

WAITING FOR HER PRINCE.

OUT where the scarlet maples grow,
   Beneath a spreading linden's shade,
   Waiting for Prince Scheherazade,
Sits pretty Katie Lamoreau.

Up in the cottage just above,
   With hard unceasing plash and rub,
   Her mother works the steaming tub,
Scrubbing and scolding, all for love.

Hard worked, hard-featured, prone to frown,
   With knitted brow and keen black eyes—
   The daughter is a sweet surprise,
The world-worn mother softened down.

And argument may not convince
   The red armed shrew that pretty Kate
   Can do aught better than to wait
Until blind fortune sends her Prince.

And she will wait each summer day,
 A senseless novel in her hand,
 Dreaming a dream of fairy land,
Until her Prince shall ride that way.

Her Prince will come ; and she will thank
 Her fortune, and be only glad,
 Tho' he is but an Irish lad,
Who wields the hod or walks the plank.

 " So, sift the classic idyls out
  From words and glosses overlaid,
 Your Damon is a Helot lout—
  Your Daphne is a chambermaid."

MAY.

THE redwinged merle, from bending spray
   On graceful pinions poising,
Pours out a liquid roundelay
   In jubilant rejoicing.
The cock-grouse drums on sounding log,
   The fox forsakes the cover,
The woodcock pipes·from fen and bog,
   From upland leas the plover.

The speckled trout dart up the stream
   Beneath the rustic bridges,
While flocks of pigeons glance and gleam
   O'er beech and maple ridges.
The golden robin trills his note
   Among the netted shadows,
The bobolink with mellow throat
   Makes musical the meadows.

The peeping frogs, with silver bells
   In rhythmical ovation,
Ring out a chime of treble swells
   In joyous gratulation.

The low of kine is mingling with
   The song of lark and sparrow,
While fallow fields are growing blithe
   Beneath the plow and harrow.

The moon all night, serene and white,
   On lake and stream is glowing,
While rippling fountains seek her light
   Through woodland valleys flowing.
And all night long a low sweet song
   Sweeps o'er the misty hollow,
From marsh and fen, from hill and glen,
   From brook, and field, and fallow.

It is the time of pleasant things,
   When Love makes up his issues,
When hearts well up like hidden springs
   From rusted cells and tissues.
A time to hear, at break of day,
   A silver-chorused matin,
A liquid fretwork in crochet,
   On atmospheric satin.

A time to feast the soul, the eyes;
   To watch each bird that passes;
And half surmise that birds are wise,
   And men are only asses.

And then, to turn and raise the load,
　　With weary shoulders bending,
And take the old, well-beaten road
　　That leads—unto the ending.

ISABEL NYE.

WHEN autumn flowers were rich in bloom
　　And ripe fruit reddened against the sky,
Through the latticed door of a maiden's room,
　　The Devil came purring to Isabel Nye.

Isabel Nye with her sun-bright face,
　　Her midnight hair, and her sloe-black eye.
Goodness, and beauty, and maiden grace,
　　Were lavished and laid on Isabel Nye.

And she had suitors who sued, for gold;
　　And lovers, who wooed for love — or lust.
But he who won her was hard and cold,
　　And he trailed her soul in the very dust.

What though my hair was a trifle gray?
 I loved her better and more than all.
I worshiped her on her queenly way,
 And her fall, to me, was an angel's fall.

Man glides to the ground by slow degrees,
 Halting and hitching at wrong or right.
But woman glissades, with fearful ease,
 Like a shooting star on a wintry night.

Ah, Isabel Nye, the winds go by;
 The beard o' the thistle sails out to sea,
And the loves of old that were like tried gold
 Have gone with the thistle-down — far a-lee.

DEACON JOHN.

Every rhythmical scribbler is entitled to one shot at the " Maud Muller " mark.   I inscribe, to the average school miss, Deacon John.

DEACON John Davis rode his mare
    Across the meadows so fresh and fair ;
Rode to a cottage, old and brown,
That stood by a brook in Lindley town,
And asked, with a shame-faced, modest mien,
For an interview with Isabel Green.
And Isabel, who had seen him come,
Said, " Tell the Deacon I ain't to hum."

For Isabel wore a Grecian bend,
And loved a young man with no end
Of soap-locks, clustering round a face
On which much hair left little space
For kissing ; while a huge mustache
Made it close work to rastle his hash.

" I think," said red-lipped Isabel Green,
"That Deacon John is real mean
To ask a girl like me t'engage
To marry a man that's twice her age."

The Deacon said, "She may be right.
I walked accordin' tu the light
I had.   I'm only thirty-eight,
And well to du, an' strong, an' straight.
I would hev let her keep the puss—
She may go furder, an' fare wuss."

And the Deacon straddled his mare agin,
Only saying, " It might hev bin."

And Isabel wedded Charley Cross,
Who ran exceedingly strong on hoss,
And made his living by little games,
From which arise unpleasant names.
He played at poker and sledge and whist,
With all the games on the gambler's list.
He fought the tiger with might and main,
And sometimes got most bitterly slain.

But then he had such eyes and hair,
And walked the streets with a princely air;
Handled his cane in a foreign style,
And had such a bandit look and smile.

Oh sweet to a silly maiden's view
Is a waxed mustache of sable hue.
And dearly the maiden loves to doat
On a handsome man in a bob-tailed coat.

But sad and sickening is the life
That waits on every gambler's wife.
And any damsel will rue the day
She marries the man who lives by play.

Isabel followed her foolish choice,
And learned to tremble at his voice.
And her soul grew sick from time to time
At the dirty deed, half trick, half crime,

As she thought of quiet Lindley town,
With its little cottage, snug and brown,
And the peaceful, healthy, happy life
She might have led as the Deacon's wife.

One night, at " Natchez under the Hill,"
It came to an end, as such things will.
There was a scrimmage — which I believe
Arose from aces, in Charley's sleeve.

No need to tell of the savage fight
That wakened the town at dead of night;
Of pistol shots, and bowies drawn,
And a shallow grave at early dawn;
But Isabel, widowed and forlorn
Went back to the spot where she was born.

And often, with thoughts too deep for words,
She watches the Deacon's flocks and herds,
Or weeps in silence to see him ride
With a blooming Deaconess at his side,
Then turns to her wash-tub once agin —
Only saying, " It might hev bin."

———

HANNAH LEE.

A Minnesota girl murdered and scalped, August, 1862.

THE prairie wind is sadly wailing,
  The ripe leaves rustle from vine and tree.
The thistle-down is softly sailing
  Above the grave of Hannah Lee.

Oh, never maiden in her dwelling
  Met fouler fate by fiendish hand,
When from his lair with beast-like yelling
  The savage burst with knife and brand.

Oh, never hair more brightly golden
  Adorned a head more sweetly fair.
Nor ever, in the ages olden,
  Walked earthly maid with queenlier air.

The brutal stake the breast impaling,
   The golden hair torn from the head —
Well may the wind, with ceaseless wailing,
   Forever mourn the queenly dead.

Far up the Athabasca's sources
   They hold the savage dance by night.
And silken hair from maiden's corses
   Gleams from the spear in fiendish rite.

The midnight fire is fiercely glowing
   On rolling stream, and rock and tree.
And from a chieftain's spear is flowing
   The golden hair of Hannah Lee.

AT ANCHOR.

I AM going a journey, brother.   Or would it be better to say,
I am just ending up a long voyage, and dropping my
kedge in the bay.
‹Coming home; and in debt to the purser, with never a dollar
to pay.

Six decades.   'Twas a wearisome voyage, made over a mystical
sea,
In a poorly rigged, plebeian lugger, that always was drifting
a-lee;
And where are the lofty square-riggers that started the voyage
with me?

They passed me far up to the windward, with stunsails aloft
and alow,
Some heading for tropical islands, some bound for the islands
of snow,
And where are the weatherly clippers the merchants delighted
to know?

Some drowsily swing to their anchors, as the meandering tides
　　go by ;
Some battle in frozen oceans, where the northerly gales are
　　high ;
Some drift in the seething tropics, with keels upturned to the
　　sky.

Oh, grand is the lofty clipper, as she dashes the yeasty brine
From the crest of the midnight billow, where the waters flash
　　and shine.
But I love the plebeian lugger—the little lugger is mine.

And lofty clipper or lugger, it comes to the same at last,
Or whether we count as wreckage, or hold to our moorings
　　fast,
When we swing to a final anchor, and the voyage of life is past.

THE CAVAN GIRL.

OH fair are Ireland's daughters, with their laughter loving
    eyes,
Their wit a constant quantity, their love a sweet surprise ;
And of all girls that walk this earth with glowing form or smile,
The fairest is the Cavan girl, the queen o' the Emerald Isle.
Her heavy tresses are blue-black, her eyes, a violet blue ;
You look far down into their depths ; in turn, they look you
    through.
Men come and go ; the seasons change ; fortune may smile,
    and pass,
Her love endures while life endures ; such is the Cavan lass.
No drunkenness nor coarse abuse can make that love abate,
Her love for once is love for aye, and cannot turn to hate.
Oh, leeze me on the Cavan girl, with eyes o' the violet shade,
And blue-black hair ; and take who will the light haired Saxon
    maid.

OLD JOHNNY JONES.

OLD Johnny Jones was a colored man,
   Wrinkled, decrepit and old.
He had an acre of arable land,
   But never a dollar in gold.
And Johnny had dwelt in the Southerners' land,
   And been coffled, and bought, and sold.

His heart was leal as the day was long,
   And he was merry and kind.
He lightened his labor with dance and song
   Until he grew lame and blind.
Then crept away from the heartless throng
   And prayed with a fervent mind.

Old Johnny has gone to his final rest,
   He has learned a loftier tune.
He passed the gates of the golden west
   On a glorious eve in June ;
And his banjo * twangs in the halls of the blest
   To a grand old Hebraic rune.

   *Johnny did not understand harps.

IN THE TROPICS.

WE cleft the waves, mound after mound,
   And still it seemed as we had not
Advanced, but when the sun went down,
   Were in the self-same spot.

Strange seabirds all the weary days
   Circled about the pilot house.
Flashing in blue and golden rays
   Bright dolphins held carouse.

The southeast trades with gentle breeze
   Swept o'er us with a breath of balm.
We only longed for land and trees,
   For homelike rest and calm.

At early morn the sea was blue,
   It still was blue at close of day.
Forever old, forever new,
   It was the same alway.

At noon we shrank beneath the sun
  That flamed in splendor overhead ;
At evening, when the day was done,
  We made the deck our bed.

We watched amid the thin pale mist
  That glimmers o'er these summer seas,
Peering through banks of amethyst
  For mangubeira trees.

And thus, at length, through seas of calm,
  And waves that changed from blue to green,
We made the blessed isles of Palm,
  With silver waves between.

We were aweary and had rest ;
  We were an hungered and were fed.
When sank the sun adown the west,
  The hammock was our bed.

At morn the humming bird was seen,
  Flashing thro' many a fairy bower,
An emerald of the brightest green,
  Set in a crimson flower.

We missed the crash and roar of trade,
  The murky mills that shriek and groan,
To smoke and swing in tropic shade,
  Where hurry is unknown.

And, though we missed the mountain breeze
　With balmy breath of feathery pines,
We found fair groves of orange trees,
　And ever flowering vines.

We missed the maids with golden curls
　And azure eyes of love and light,
But danced and sang with dark haired girls
　Whose eyes were just as bright.

We missed the northern star at night,
　We missed the cooling breeze at morn ;
We missed the slowly waning light,
　The fields of waving corn.

Oh clear and pure the stars may shine,
　And brighter than in northern lands ;
And gorgeous flowers may deck the vine
　That sweeps the silver sands ;

And rich and rare the birds may be
　That gem the banks of Amazon,
And bright the sheen of vine and tree,
　With golden fruit upon ;

But dull stagnation, like a pall,
　Hangs o'er the land so fair and frail ;
It is the Serpent land—and all
　Bear witness of the trail.

What wonder if we came to long,
   Or that the longing daily grew,
For northern birds in silvery song,
   And lakes of limpid blue.

What wonder if the gay macaws
   Gave less delight than homely birds,
Or that we tired of Romish laws,
   And longed for Saxon words.

PARA, NORTH BRAZIL, June 10, 1867.

THE MAMELUCO DANCE.

'TWAS night, and bowered amid tall, feathery palms,
    Belem the Beautiful by moonlight slept,
And o'er the red-tiled roofs that lay aslant,
Flecked with the swaying shadow of the trees,
Came faint, low music, and the rhythmic chime
Of many feet, that, through the tropic night,
Untired, untiring, shook the trellised vines
That veiled the lattice windows ; and the voice,
Wild, pleading, passionate, of him who played
The primitive zambrina, broke at times
Upon the midnight cadence of wild sounds,
And as the pleading passion of his song
Came o'er the dancers, one and all joined in
For a brief verse, and a low wail arose,
And passed away, as 'twere a spirit's cry.
Idly I swung my hammock to and fro,
Wooing the sleep that came not. What to me
Were Mameluco dances ? What cared I·
For wild Cabano songs that mourned the time
When Vinagre and Malcher led the hosts
Of the Cabanos, and the streets that slept

So peacefully by moonlight were the scenes
Of butcheries at which the soul recoils?
Or what to me the desolate wail of those
Who mourned the dusky warriors from the isles
Of Amazonas?   And I turned and strove
To shut all thought of wild Cabano chiefs,
All sound of song or dance, far out of mind.
In vain.   For, ever as the silence fell,
The constant, low, unceasing monotone
Of the zambrina smote upon the ear,
Mixed with the chiming cadence of the dance.
While ever and anon the passionate wail
Of the Cabano chorus, in a key,
Minor and mournful, thrilled my northern blood
To most unwonted heat.

     Why should I strive
For sleep that would not come?   Here was a phase
Of human life and passion, little known
To all the many writers whose deft pens
Have chronicled the wonders and wild scenes
Of Amazonas.   I arose and donned
Such clothing as a northerner may need
Within the tropics.   Lightest fabrics serve,
In this warm clime, so that they be but clean,
And worn, ev'n as the morals of the land,
Loosely but gracefully.

I sought the gate,

And was admitted by a courtly slave

Whose bow had won the heart of Chesterfield.

A rustic house, whose many-latticed walls

Gave freest scope to all of air that stirred

Beneath the swaying palms. A heavy door,

Swinging ajar to such as might approach

With courteous word and mien. An earthen floor ;

A long, quaint room, and latticed-windows, where

Strange vines and gorgeous roses intertwined

Sighed to the soft sea-breeze. A scent of flowers,

Faint but delicious; and a dusky band

Of rude musicians, who all night kept up

The tune untiring, with the startling wail

Of Tupi chorus changefully thrown in.

A medley of wild faces and lithe forms ;

A waving sea of dancers, whose free grace

Was like the leisure of a petted swan.

And much of simple love, and courtesy

That seemed a thing inborn, were shown by all.

Hard by the door that opened to the hall,

There stood a broad, low-spreading palm whose shade

Made blackest midnight; and, from underneath

The feathery leaves a scowling face with dark,

And serpent eyes, peered ever and anon

Within the room, watching the changing dance

Much as a waiting python eyes his prey.

The evil, vengeful face was naught to me,

Yet, such a face once seen will haunt the soul,

Like the vague trouble of a shapeless dream.

I joined the dusky throng, and straightway felt

The wild, strange chorus stir my Saxon blood,

As when a cry, of anguish wakes the ear

Upon the middle of the quiet night.

It was a simple measure that they danced,

Well suited to the drowsy monotone

Of the zambrina, played by native hands,

Save when the chorus rose, and Malcher's name

Raised Tupi blood to frenzy.   Then they swayed

As bends the forest to a sudden gale,

Dancing with tight clasped hands, and eager eyes

Bent on the roof above ;—a moment thus,

Then, as the wail died out, they once again

Resumed the easy step and languid mien,

While glances from dark eyes, and meaning looks

Changed with the changing mazes of the dance.

There is a nameless charm about these girls,

With their dark eyes, and masses of black hair

Falling disheveled over shapely neck

And bust a duchess might be proud to own.

A grace of mien and manner, seldom seen

Where fashion sets the bounds, and stiff-backed men

Bow, after a set form, to courtly dames,
Who sink all lines of female grace, to grace
A graceless fashion of a graceless time.

Among the dancers there were two who stood
Pre-eminent o'er all the rest, in form,
In feature, and the nameless winning charm
That makes Eve's sons and daughters lovable.
The one, a dusky maiden from the isle
Of Oncas; lithe and tall, with waving hair,
Ink-black, and falling o'er, in glossy waves,
A pair of shoulders, such as might have graced
The love of Anthony for Egypt's queen.
Her mate, a dark eyed Vaquero, who roamed
A lord among the herds of Marajo.
I only noted that he had a form
Of manly comeliness, vouchsafed to few;
A fierce, free manner, such as suits with those
Who throw the lasso, and whose lives are passed
Among wild beasts and wilder, fiercer men,
Upon the treeless campos. Courteous too,
He was; but that is little in a land
Where courtesy is natural to all.
These two, the maiden and her cavalier,
Had eyes or words but for each other. One
May find such cases in the land where suns
Are hot and constant, and the sultry clime

Sends mischief coursing through the veins of men
No less than women.

                  Two short days before,
And he who scowled beneath the spreading palm
Had sought the favor of the queenly girl
In vain.   Her love was lavished on the man
Who wore the scarlet sash and silver spurs
That mark a rider chief of Marajo.

'Twas in the small hours of the early morn,
When wearied with the dance they paused to rest
And drink, as is their wont, and raise the song
And wailing chorus for the dusky dead
Who sleep in nameless graves along the banks
Where Alta Amazonas meets the sea.
The song was of the rudest ; yet it had
A simple pathos, such as may be heard
Where'er the Tupi tongue is understood,
Or the Tapuyo treasures up his wrongs,
To pour them out in wild impassioned rhythm.
And there was something in the mournful wail
That spoke the cadenced language of despair.
No savan I, nor skilled in any tongue
Save the plain English that I learned to lisp
Beside a mother's knee.   If I translate
Too rudely or too freely, be the fault

On me, and me alone.   The Vaquero,
With rich, deep voice that suited well the man,
Chanted the body of the simple song,
While all joined in the chorus, and the wail
Rose like a Celtic *Keenah* for the dead.

TUPI LAMENT.

We sing the noble dead to-night
  Who sleep in jungle covered graves,
We sing the brave who fell in fight
  Beside the Amazona's waves,
The white man counts us with his beasts,
And makes our girls the slaves of priests.
  Woe, woe for the Cabano !

Our war canoes came down the stream,
  We stormed their hosts at Cam-e-ta ;
Obidos saw our lances gleam.
  We swept their forces at Para,
But English ships were on the waves.
And still our girls are serfs and slaves.
  Woe, woe for the Cabano !

We drove them from the Tocantins,
  We swept them from the Tapajoz.
A feeble race with feeble means,
  Our courage conquered all our foes.

NOTE.—Cabanos, dwellers in cabins.

But English ships and English men
Have made us serfs and slaves again.
  Woe, woe for the Cabano!

We were a fierce avenging flood
  That no Brazilian force could stem.
We reddened all their towns with blood,
  From Onca's isle to Santarem,
But ah, our best are in their graves
And we again are serfs and slaves!
  Woe, woe for the Cabano!

Accursed be the war canoe
  That bore the wily Joachim;
And God requite the Mundurucu
  Who slew our sires at Santarem.
For on their heads shall rest the guilt
Of Indian blood by Indians spilt.
  Woe, woe for the Cabano!

The song was ended, and the dancers stood
With hands upraised and eyes turned heavenward,
When he who watched beneath the spreading palm
Entered the room with swift and noiseless tread,
Stole on the dancers with an Onca's step,
Dealt on the Vaquero two swift, light blows
That fell between the clavicle and ear,

Then vanished into darkness with a speed
That mocked pursuit. 'Twas done so quietly,
So quickly, and the blows were such mere taps,
That I could scarcely deem the whole a thing
Of serious import ; but, I wronged the man.
He had more skill in murder than I thought.

The Vaquero with quick, convulsive start,
Flashed from its sheath a keen Damascene blade,
But all too late.   The murderer was away.
And the bright life blood welled in crimson jets,
While, drawn to his full height, the rider stood
A moment, as the scarlet tide o'erflowed
The velvet doublet, gaudy sash, and thence
Adown the wide slashed trowsers to the spurs;
Then slowly sank upon the earthen floor,
With head soft pillowed on the swelling breast
That wrought his ruin.

                        'Twas a ghastly sight.
The queenly maiden with her snowy robes
Drenched crimson in the life-blood of the man
Who held her heart.   Wildly she strove to staunch
The intermitting tide that kept strange pace
With every heart-beat, lavishing meanwhile
Terms of endearment and wild words of love
Upon the dying man, whose paling lips
Answered with love again.

       Short shrift had he.

Two gaping wounds, the least of which might let

The strongest life out in a short half hour,

Soon sped him on the road whence none return.

The well turned head, with its broad, open brow,

Sank heavy on the blood bespattered breast

That beat for him alone. The ashy lips

Strove vainly to articulate a prayer,

Or, it might be, a last fond word of love ;

But, even as he strove, with gasping breath

The soul went out.

      There was the usual fuss

That Latin races make about their dead.

Firstly a priest, with shaven crown and dull,

Lack-luster eye, mumming some papish rite

O'er the unheeding clay. A surgeon next,

Striving to split the difference which lay

Betwixt his dignity and need of haste.

Also, he may have been somewhat in doubt

About his fee. Then the police, who made

An absurd pretense of awakened zeal,

Searching vine-covered arbors and old walls,

Peering in ruined buildings, and about

The orange groves and gardens, knowing well

The man was in the jungle, and they might

With equal thrift attempt to ferret out

A needle in a field of drifting sand.

Two ancient negresses with staring eyes,
Long, skinny arms, and hands like vultures' claws,
Removed the clotted blood and dried the floor.
Four Topugos bore off the murdered man,
Preceded by the priest, and at his side
The maiden, in her blood-bedraggled robes.
The dancers took their places as before ;
And, as I sought my hammock, there arose
The same zambrina's tinkling monotone,
Timing the rhythmic tread of dancing feet.

A TROPICAL SCRAP.

FRONTING the casa, where I swing
   My hammock in this sultry clime,
There comes the low, unceasing chime
Of Southern folk, who dance and sing.

I hear strange cries of bird and beast,
   I hear faint chimes from Ma-ca-pa ;
   I see faint lights that gleam afar,
I watch the moon rise in the east ;

The tropic moon, that northern eyes
   May never see so near, or bright,
   And tropic fire-flies, whose strange light,
Through the dark hours will sink and rise.

MARAJO, NORTH BRAZIL, Sept. 20, 1870.

TYPEE.

A THOUSAND leagues from the clime of snow,
  In an evergreen isle in a coral sea,
Where the bread-fruit tree and the cocoanut grow,
  Is the dreamy and beautiful vale of Typee.

The reign of summer is ever there,
  Ever the waters like crystal flow;
Dreamily, balmily sleeps the air
  On lilies in clusters, like banks of snow.

Adown the valley a sparkling brook
  O'er silvery pebbles winds its way
By many a shady evergreen nook,
  To the coral waves of a land-locked bay.

Up the stream, in the soothing shade,
  Its waters expand in a glassy pool,
And hither comes each Typeean maid
  To bathe in its waters so clear and cool.

And nut-brown naiads, with swan-like ease
   Flash through the water like rays of light,
Or roam together these groves of peace
   To weave bright garlands for heads as bright.

And forms that are cast in beauty's mold,
   Glowing with vigor, in action free,
Display ripe charms more precious than gold.
   Such are the maids of the vale of Typee.

TO GEN. T. L. YOUNG.

BECAUSE my soul is weary, and
    For that old days come back in dreams,
  With visions of cool mountain streams
That bubble in a northern land;

And that I tire of palms and vines,
  And hate the papaguyo's squall,
  And long for apples in the fall
And hunter camps, and breath of pines;

And that my soul is sick to-day,
  With waiting on a trifling race
  Where oily tongue and smiling face
Are prone to palter and betray;

And that I do remember all
  Old friends with whom I walked the lines
  Y-blazed on beechen trees or pines,
And every pool or waterfall

Where crimson spotted trout would rise;
  And that I watch the hours away
  For white winged ships from New York Bay
Whose striped flags bear starry eyes—

For these, and for the thoughts that stir
   Within me, I will slaughter time
   And break the limping legs of rhyme,
Garrulous of the days that were.

Far down the bay, on either hand
   I see the sleeping islands lie
   In beauty, underneath a sky
Bluer than in our northern land.

A living scroll of evergreen
   Sweeps downward to the sluggish stream,
   Where gorgeous insects flash and gleam
Like gems, athwart the vernal sheen.

By Ma-ca-pa the crisp waves curl
   Where music sounds the whole night long,
   And wild Cabano dance and song
Are done by dark-haired Muri girls.

There dusky maids bedecked with flowers
   Dance under mangubeira trees,
   And indolence, and love, and ease
Make up the sum of tropic hours.

The firelight gleams on eyes of jet
   And maiden breasts of nuttiest brown,
   Slow palpitating up and down,
Like summer waves that heave and set.

The hidden tropic fire I see
　Flash out in every dusky face ;
　But I am of a manlier race,
And these are naught to mine or me.

And soon I take the watery plain
　Where many a white winged ship has sailed
　For home.　And some have fought and failed,
In fierce typhoon or hurricane.

　　T　　　　T

And so—for that my heart is sick—
　I write to him who left in fee
　The whiskey bottle in the tree,
Far up the forks of Freeman Creek.

PARA, NORTH BRAZIL, Oct., 1870.

ROSES OF IMEEO.

THE sun is bright in other climes,
  And bright the crystal waters flow.
The trees as gently woo the wind,
  As sweetly rare the roses grow ;
But ah, within our northern climes
They only bloom at fitful times.

Listless, I sit and watch the waves
  As drowsily they ebb and flow,
Fresh from the coral groves and caves '
  About the Isle of Imeeo,
And wonder how I could exist
In sleet and snow, and northern mist.

All day the sun shines warm and bright,
  Be it December, March, or June.
And damask roses court the sight
  At dewy morn or drowsy noon.
For in no other land will grow
Such roses as on Imeeo.

Inland a league there sleeps a vale,

    The mystic valley of Martair,

Where nut-brown maids weave lilies pale

    And roses, in their dusky hair,

And fairy forms and starry eyes

    Dance underneath cerulean skies.

A DREAM OF THE TROPICS.

I DREAMED that I dwelt in the brightest of climes
    And the fairest of isles, in a tropical sea.
Where summer extends, thro' all seasons and times,
    Her loveliest smiles over blossom and tree;

That the skies of the isle were invitingly blue;
    That the birds were of plumage the richest and rarest.
That sweetly and gently the soft falling dew
    Kissed orange tree blossoms and lilies the fairest.

I dreamed that the maids of the isle were as fair
    As the goddess of love when she rose from the ocean,
With love-lighted eyes and a wealth of dark hair,
    That might claim from a poet a life-long devotion;

That I wandered at night by the light of the moon
  With bright laughing girls, thro' the spice scented groves,
Or dreamily sailed o'er the glassy lagoon,
  And slumbered afloat in the star-lighted coves.

'Twas a dream, and it passed.   I awoke with the dawn ;
  Coldly awoke to the hard and the real,
The snow deeply drifting on meadow and lawn
  Dispelled all too quickly my fairy ideal.

I have wandered since then in those tropical seas,
  On coral reefed islands have tarried full long ;
But I found that the zephyrs were fraught with disease,
  And the paradise birds were all wanting in song.

DESILUSAO.

TO-DAY I go aside to weep —
  To play the woman with mine eyes,
 As one who in his anguish cries
For rest, and everlasting sleep.

The weary seasons went and came,
  And hairs were getting thin and gray,
  While, in a secret, quiet way,
I wrought for what were wealth and fame.

At length my plans approached the turn
  Where culmination waits on hope ;
  And, only asking trial scope,
I said, Approach, and see, and learn.

And men, suspending judgment till
  The proofs were ripe, looked on and said,
  "He has not wrought with level head —
His plans looked well, they ripen ill."

And they said well.   The truth is true,
   And men, God wot, are mainly just.
   Whatever is, whatever must
Be true, they take—but not on trust.

And I bow down ; and only pray· ·
   That others, better counting cost,
   May rightly win where I have lost,
And straighten where I went astray.

And having lost ten years of life
   Attempting what was not to be,
   I find myself again at sea,
With bread to win for child and wife.

This only.   And a single day
   I give to solitude and grief
   That the swelled heart may find relief—
And then to labor—as I may.

AN ARKANSAS IDYL.

Suggested by newspaper accounts of a Southern family feud, in which the adult males on either side were nearly exterminated—the feud being finally settled by intermarriage.

IN a half decayed log cabin, on the shore of Apple Lake,
  Dwelt a lank, ill-favored squatter by the name of Poker
    Jake,
(Which his real name was Likens), and he raised a motley crew
Of tow-headed sons and daughters, as such fellows mostly do,
Without culture or good manners, and with no regard for law,
Trained to loafing, drinking, fighting, and to fish and shoot and
    chaw.

Seven miles below Old Likens, by a marshy, muddy sloo,
At the turning of the river, lived Old Simmons and his crew;
And as between the fathers or the sons of either gang,
It would be very hard to say which most deserved to hang.
And yet, though they were ornery, it must be freely owned,
They were exceeding chivalric—surprisingly high-toned.
One of them might abstract a horse, or rob the mail by night—
But just insinuate he lied—he'd slice you up on sight.

Now, old man Likens had a mule, a spike-tailed smoky gray,
Which Ikey Simmons found at large, and claimed it as a stray,
And took it off and sold it, and pocketed the dust,
Which filled the tribe of Poker Jake with anger and disgust.
Then Yancey Likens took his gun and sallied out alone,
And soon the tribe of Simmons had a funeral of their own.

Such summary proceedings in a rural neighborhood
Produce unpleasant feelings, and result in nothing good.
For David Simmons took his gun, and lay for Poker Jake,
And shot him, catching catties, in a dugout on the lake.

Then all the neighbors felt that this had gone too deep for fun,
And that a deadly quarrel had undoubtedly begun.
For Yancey Likens at the grave was heard to swear aloud,
He'd lay for every Simmons and exterminate the crowd!
It was a rash expression, and could only be condoned
By the fact that he was fiery, and uncommonly high-toned.
Likewise he was the coolest man, and hardest shot by odds—
He had been known to hit a deer at five and forty rods.

The Simmons cabin faced the sloo, with just a path between,
And on the other side came down the forest, dense and green.
And just within the forest's edge, beside a sycamore,
Did Yancey Likens take his stand, to watch the cabin door.
And when he saw old Simmons come meandering round the
    sloo,
He took a rest across a log, and bored him through and through!

Old Simmons had a daughter—Martha Washington by name,
A round-limbed, blue-eyed, handsome jade, of most decided
    game.
And she had loved this Yancey—but that was over now—
She took a shotgun from its hooks, and registered a vow.
She loaded up both barrels with the biggest kind of shot,
And went gunning after Yancey.   Yancey, he got up and got.
He was as brave in single fight as any man unhung,
But could he harm the girl he loved, so brave, so fair and
    young?

And so, although she prowled around, and hid beside the road,
And bushwhacked every cowpath that led to his abode,
And though Ma'am Likens got a charge of bird shot in a place
That caused her to repose at night by lying on her face,
And though old granny Simmons, picking chips beside her door,
Got hit just where Ma'am Likens had been hit the week before,
And though Andrew Jackson Likens got a bullet in his thigh,
She could get no shot at Yancey.   Yancey held his hand too
    high.
Perhaps if Yancey chose to tell, he might explain just how
It happened no one shot at her in all this precious row.

But, anyway, she had her way, and played the Indian scout,
Until one afternoon, when strength and pluck were giving out,
She sought a quiet spot, and scraping leaves into a heap,
But meaning still to keep awake, dropped calmly off to sleep,

And dreamed her love dream o'er again, and that 'twas early
  spring,
And Yancey Likens came to her, and brought the wedding ring.
But when he strove to put it on, she saw it, with alarm,
Expand, and slip above her hand, and rest upon her arm.
And then the ring began to shrink, until it grew so tight,
The sharp compression caused her pain, and woke her in a
  fright.
And then she saw, with sudden fear, a pair of brawny fists,
That most uncompromisingly imprisoned both her wrists!

She fought like any mountain cat, and in her struggles swore
She never had been so misused by any man before.
She wrenched herself as she had been an acrobat on show,
And shrieked, "You low-down, ornery pup, how dar you
  squeeze me so!"
But still the iron grip remained, and o'er her shoulders fell
The steady gaze of steel-gray eyes—the eyes she knew so well!
A laughing face looked down on hers, and all in vain she tried
To free herself, and then—and then she wilted down and cried.

Ma'am Likens, with a water-gourd, went hobbling to the spring.
She was too old and lame to dance—too cussed mad to sing.
She crooned and grumbled in her wrath, until she met her son,
A-galivanting down the path, with Martha Washington!

No matter how they compromised each ugly word and deed —
Young Yancey had the leading mind—and leading minds will
  lead.

They sent young Thomas Benton Likens off to bring a priest,
Likewise, a keg of applejack—ten gallons at the least.
The tribe of Simmons all came up—the Likenses were there,
The neighbors swore they ne'er before had seen a bride so fair.*
Young Yancey led the festive dance, with Martha at his side,
While Montagues and Capulets pranced after them with pride.
Ma'am Likens, primed with applejack, went halting thro' a reel,
While Granny Simmons in her chair kept time with toe and
     heel.

They smoked the fragrant cob of peace, they drank their toddy
     hot,
They swore an everlasting truce and sealed it on the spot,
By digging underneath a tree a narrow grave and deep,
And burying the tomahawk where Martha went to sleep

-----

*This was written years before Joaquin Miller's "William Brown, of
Oregon," saw the light.

THE SCALP HUNTER IS INTERVIEWED.

"YES, I'm the man you're talkin' about, the Brute that
murders the Soos
On the upper Athabasca; an' you kin tell 'em the news
Down East, where they print the Tribune, and the Quaker peo-
ple blow
About the wrongs of the Red man. It's cursed little they know
About the wrongs of the White man, for you want to recollect
Thet a white man hez no rights which a red is bound to
respect.

So, they've got me into the papers; and I am a 'Fiend,' and
'whar
I find a squaw or a papoose, I shoot 'em an' raise the har?'

It's tol'able true, I reckon. As sure as you're alive,
I've hunted them dev'lish redskins, till I've scalped some thirty-
five!

Wouldn't 'a thought I could done it? Well, the yarn *is* middlin'
tough,
For the devils are mighty cunnin' an' the country is cold an'
rough,

An' I was alone for the most part. There was three of us at
    the start ;
But they shot Jim Biddle one mornin', with an arrer, thro' the
    heart.

An' we had to cache for safety, Tom Burlingame an' me,
For the Soos war right upon us, an' Tom was hit in the knee

An' *couldn't* run. So, seein' our fix, it seemed more wise
To cache in a pra'rie dugout, an' sell at the goin' price.

We played our hands right lively ; killed seven, did Tom an' I,
Besides a few that was gut-shot, an' hid in the grass to die.

But they played it low down on us ; heaped pra'rie grass an'
    sticks
About our den an' smoked us out. 'Twas one of their Injun
    tricks.

No use to tell how they flanked us with their blasted savage fun,
Makin' us run the ga'ntlet—only Tom, he couldn't run.

So they tied him with buff'ler lariats to a stake driv' in the
    ground,
An' roasted him by a slow fire, while they hooted an' danced
    around. ·

They cut out his tongue, cut his ears off, then keerfully saved
    his har
By peelin' the scalp—it's a wonder what a mountain man kin
    bar

Without peepin'; an' Tom was bully ; quiet, silent, an' grim.
They tried all manner of torments, but never a yelp from him.

He died as game as a badger.   They 'lowed to keep me a spell,
Then git up an Injun pow-wow, an' give me special hell.

An' they would 'a done it certain, for I was cowed an' lame,
But Sheridan's men war on it, an' blocked that little game.

Bust into the camp one mornin', an' scattered the gang like
        chaff,
Killed an' wounded a hundred.—Oh no, *I* didn't laugh !

' Providential,' was it ?   Don't seem to see it that way.
Sheridan giv' the order—soldiers mostly obey.

Good fellers, them boys o' Sheridan's ; they did the handsome
        thing,
Cured me up an' fitted me out for another start in spring.

Giv' me a navy Colt, a knife, an' rifle, an' hoss,
Told me to raise the har of every Soo I kem across,

An' I've mostly done it.   'Git me ?'   Of course the game'll turn.
But I shall go under fightin',—I aint a-goin' to burn ;

I've seen that once too often.   An' stranger, don't talk too loud
When you tell of the old scalp hunter some day to an Eastern
        crowd.

Remember thar ain't no story but is bound to hev two sides,
And thar's reason for every bullet I stick in their blasted hides.

For *I* had a wife an' children, which the same was dear to me,
Murdered in Minnesota, the year of the massa*cree.*

I might hev stood the killin', though *hit* was savage enougn—
But stakiu' a woman down to the ground is playin' it dev'lish
    rough.

The way they murdered my little gals of twelve an' fourteen
    years—
No matter—swearin' is too thin, an' I don't run to tears,

They blur the eyes for shootin'.   But mebbe you might git riled,
If I told you the sickenin' trick they played my wife an' unborn
    child.

I found her out on the pra'rie with a stake drove through her
    breast,
An' the babe right on her bosom.—Perhaps you can guess the
    rest.

'Twas a hellish sight for a father. My heart froze hard right thar.
I dried clean down to ugliness, an' went in wicked for har.

I've panned 'em down to the bed-rock, 'n' I reckon afore I've
    done,
The scalps of my wife an' children will bring me twenty for one.

And when you write to the papers, if you want to mention me,
Remember Minnesota, and tell of the massa*cree.*

THE BANSHEE OF McBRIDE.

IN the Island of Unreason, where the bog is green and wet,
  Where no sequences of reason prove a consequence, or
    debt;
Where deductions from equations are derided or denied,
And the table of the multiples is laughed at and decried,
Stands a mud and granite edifice, the Castle of McBride.

And of all the brave old families that date from King O'Toole,
The ancient lines of Donohue, O'Grady or McDhoul,
O'Neil, O'Brien, or Callahan, or Murphy or Burnside,
No one could show a pedigree or date like The McBride.

No ancient Irish family from Kerry to Tyrone
Would be complete unless it had a Banshee of its own;
And of all the howling Banshees that wailed o'er storm and
    tide,
The loudest and the shrillest was the Banshee of McBride.

'Tis midnight, and the festive board is loud with drink and
    song;
Lord Hugh is at his bravest, and the sitting will be long.

The punch is strong, the wit is keen—the storm may beat the
    pane—
When did the Lord O' the Castle heed wind, or tide, or rain?

But o'er the scene there comes a voice that bates the revelers'
    breath,
A wailing, long-drawn, moaning cry, that speaks of doom and
    death.
And as all eyes are looking to the master of the feast,
Lord Hugh arises slowly, turning sadly to the east

Like an ancient necromancer. And he spoke in solemn words
Of the old Milesian legends, and the voice of prophet birds,
And how the grand ould families, the proudest of the land,
Had been forewarned by mystic signs that none might under-
    stand.

And then his lordship mixed the punch, and as he passed the
    bowl,
Says he "whoever this may call, may heaven absolve his soul."

Old Katy Nolan, broiling bones to keep the drinkers dry,
She crossed herself in deadly fear to hear the Banshee's cry.
She raised the keenah and bewailed, "Och, wirra, wirrasthrue,
Who can the Banshee want this night—can it be Masther Hugh?

"Or is it Shamus, or mad Tom—who can it mane at all?
(Sure, 'twouldn't be Miss Ellen, the life an' light o' the hall.)

"Av it wor Masther Shamus, the blagyard who has spint
A foine estate, an' ruined all the income and the rint—
Och hone, he is the bravest lad, an' spirited an' kind—
He rides the horses all to death, an' niver rides behind ;
He sits the longest at the dhrink, he's first in dance or fight —
But Och, a bigger blagyard doesn't walk the earth this night.

"Or av 'twor Masther Thomas, the nuisance of the Hall,
Who's always ready at the dhrink, an' always first to fall—
He spends his money like a prince—whene'er he has to spind—
(Bad luck to thim ould misers, that is so afeard to lind.)

"Mayhap 'twould be Ould Teddy—the ouldest of the stock,
An' him bed-rid sence Candlemas, by rayson of the shock.
Av it *is* him—O howly saints, dale lightly for his sake —
There's not an Irish gintleman could have a grander wake."

Old Terence lay upon his cot, a withered, wasted form.
He heard the Banshee's wailing cry above the crashing storm,
And calling, in a feeble voice, O'Brien to his side,
He said, "My lad, ye soon will see the last of The McBride.
Go down an' spake to James an' Hugh, an' say the ould man
        thinks
This night will be his last on earth—an' don't forget the
        dhrinks."

And soon the ancient family came thronging to his door,
Except young Tom—the blackguard—who lay drunk upon the
        floor.

They propped him up with pillows, with the punch in easy
    reach,
And listened while with trembling lips he màde his dying
    speech.

THE SPEECH.

Jist touch the whiskey to me lips—arrah, I shan't be long.
Shamus, my boy, what ails the punch ?   You've wathered it too
   · strong.
'Tis wather spoils the best of dhrink—or have I lost me taste ?
(O'Brien, take the cart, an' bring his riverence, the praste.)

Och hone ! 'tis eighty years an' more I lived on this estate,
An' never once oppressed the poor, or bowed before the great.
An' tho' the property was spint long years before it came
To me, I held it like a prince, an' you may do the same.

Remember honor is yer life, an' never take the lie
From any man, an' never be afraid to fight, or die.
And kape the brave ould customs good, an' let the whiskey flow
At Christmas, christenings, an' wakes ; an' as for friend an' foe,
Turn a bould face to both o' thim.—An' never pay a debt—
Onless ye pay a laborer, or praste, or honest bet.
(The moneylendhers all are thaives.) An' kape yer shootin' fine
By practice, and the steady hand that comes of punch an' wine.

Presarve the game ; an' whin the leaves are rustlin' on the
 ground,
Remember there is other game, that lasts the sayson round,
The partridge is in feather whin the lanes are brown an' sere—
But the bailiff and the gauger are in sayson all the year.

I lave this fine ould mansion as I found it. There is much
That English laws would rendher to the moneylendhers' touch.
I held the place for sixty years. I kep' it as I could—
'Twill hould another sixty years—for thim as makes it good.

I've said my say—*Sanctissima.* My spache is gettin' thick—
An' here comes Father Shaughnessy—pass round the punch,
 avie."

So passed away this brave old man, a real Irish Prince,
Whom logic could not turn aside, nor argument convince.
And he was right. He held his lands long after they were
 spent ;
He gathered all his friends around, he gathered all the rent.
He walked according to his light, and in his narrow way
Absorbed much antique salary and antedated pay
Let us be mindful of his deeds, and thankful for his sake,
That no old Irish gentleman e'er had a grander wake.

HOW MIAH JONES GOT DISCOURAGED.

MIAH JONES was a powerful man, whose delight was a personal tussle.

He could travel, if any one can, on his individual muscle.

And he often remarked in his tramps, he wished some kind fortune would bring him

A man who would ante the stamps, and endeavor to lick him or fling him.

Daniel Rawson lived on a small farm, some twenty-two miles south of Wooster,

And few had a leg or an arm like this agricultural rooster.

He had heard of the bragging of Miah, but never had happened to know him;

And he said, "'f I was younger an' spryer, I'll bet I could lick him or throw him."

Now, when Miah heard of this talk, he started right off for a visit,

But happened to meet in his walk a sort of bucolic "what is it?"

Which the same was a load of dry hay, meandering over the
    gravel,

And Miah was puzzled to say what caused such a haystack to
    travel.

For there was no wagon nor team, yet the haystack kept
    silently going

Like a lumbering ark on a stream, or a lazy old darkey-man
    mowing.

But a voice came from under the load, at which Miah con-
    su-med-ly wondered,

Saying, "They've loaded me up for a ton, and they've cheated
    me out of three hundred,

Or my name ain't Rawson."

                    Then Miah

Walked pensively off from that image.

MORAL.

For a gruffy old pill
    What can carry a ton
Up a gravelly hill
    Ain't exactly the one
That you want to pick up for a scrimmage.

GREETING TO THE DEAD.

WHERE the scarlet balm blossoms are nodding and
    swaying,
Where a cool crystal brooklet is rippling and straying,
A dusky-eyed infant is gleefully playing,
Singing and playing the long summer day.

Where the shade of the maple is waving and flitting,
Wearily sewing, or cutting and fitting,
Over the way, by the window, is sitting
A widow, in weeds of the dreariest gray.

Down where the Father of Waters is flowing,
Where orange trees bloom and the south wind is blowing,
Down where the war-ships are coming and going
To valorous deeds of the loyal and free,

Sleepeth the husband and father.   Quiescent
He rests in his grave, where the waves iridescent
Gild steeple and tower in the once haughty Crescent,
That stands where the waters sweep down to the sea.

Soul that no treason nor guile could inveigle,
Dying in patience and pride that was regal,
Firm hand of the fearless, bright eye of the eagle,
A greeting we send to thy grave by the sea.

NEW YEAR'S ODE.—1866.

THE Old must perish that the New may live,
 And what the Old hath lacked, the New shall give.
The bugle's bray and crash of rolling drums
Have ceased to weary, and the New Year comes
Laden with promise, rich with budding hopes
Of all men value most, while treason gropes
In outer darkness, striving still to save
Some barbarous relic from its traitor grave,
Fierce to oppress, eager to crush the right,
Arrogant still, though baffled in the fight,
Sullenly pettifogging for the wrong,
And slow to common justice.   Not for long
Shall this endure ; the nation's blood has bought
The precious boon of liberty, and naught
That treason dares or foreign foes may do
Shall bar its progress.   As the years run through
Their changing seasons, brighter still shall grow
The radiant goddess Freedom, who, although
Her path be strewn with wrecks and martyrs' bones,
Shall still march on o'er empires, kings and thrones.

Ring out to-day a merry peal
   From every belfry in the land,
   Till every child may understand
And every loyal heart shall feel
That Freedom has a truer birth,
   A prouder right ; and we may claim
   The foremost place, the highest name
Among the nations of the earth.

Our bitter trial days are past ;
   And rich red blood that flowed like rain
   Has not been poured to earth in vain.
Peace settles on the land at last,
And yule logs burn, while those who grieve
   Shall gather round the Christmas fires
   Where gladdened mothers, sons and sires,
Meet on this happy New Year's eve.

To night beneath the glinting stars
   Full many a voice shall ring with mirth,
   While gathered round the social hearth
We half forget the nation's scars.
And many a mother's lip shall smile
   Whose heart is with the dead to-night,
   And many a maiden's eye grow bright
Whose soul is sick with grief the while.

BALLAD OF YE LEEK HOOK.

OR, THE POTTER COUNTY VOLUNTEER.

It is probably known to all well informed people that, in the early days of
Potter County, Pa., the food of the inhabitants consisted mainly of trout, veni-
son, and leeks. For convenience in digging leeks, a long spur, something like
an old-fashioned bayonet, was (or might have been) worn on the heel.

A BOLD young raftsman dwelt among the Potter County
pines.

He had no shade trees round his hut, nor any flowers, nor vines,

But yet he had a gallant heart, and when the war began

He swore that he could whip Old Jeff—or any other man.

And he has sold his brindle cow, likewise his yaller dog,

And left his double bitted ax a stickin' in the log ;

Has donned his brightest scarlet shirt.   "And now," says he,
    " I shall

Jest take a walk to Lungerville, and have a talk with Sal."

When gentle Sally saw him come, she dropped her gathered
    leeks,

Her waterfall came tumbling down—the roses left her cheeks ;

"Oh John," she cried, "you're all drest up, an' I know what
    it's for,

You're 'listed for a volunteer—you're goin' up to war!"

"Oh Sally, dry your lovely eyes, an' do not be afraid,
But bear thee gallantly, as should a Potter County maid ;
And give to me some trifling thing—a token, ere I go,
That I may wear it as a badge in presence of the foe."

Then stooped the lovely blushing maid, and from her tiny heel
Unstrapped a wondrous instrument, a shining spur of steel ;
And "Wear thou this," the damsel said ; "for it shall be thy
     shield,
The talisman against all harm upon the battle field."

Oh many a field in Dixie's Land and many a Southland stream
Have seen that fearless volunteer—that leek hook's awful gleam.
And soon the Johnnies learned to say, "There comes the cussed
     Yank,
Who wears a bayonet on his heel, and strikes us in the flank."

At Malvern Hill, at Gettysburg, and at the Seven Pines,
That fearful leek hook flashed like fire along the rebel lines.
"Because," said John, "I hold it true, that any man of nerve
Can kill more Rebs to go it on his individual curve."

And so for three long years he fought, o'er many a weary mile,
Killing six general officers, with scores of rank and file,
For wheresoe'er that leek hook flashed, by river, hill or plain,
'Twas there the fiercest fighting was—the biggest heaps of
     slain !

All honor to the shining blade that digs the fragrant root,
Yet makes a fearful weapon on a Potter County foot.
All honor to our soldiers who the rebel cause have smashed—
And let us pray that John and Sal may run together—lashed.

KING COTTON.

ALAS for the snow-white king, the milk-white feathery king,
   Who sat on a Southland throne, and ruled by the chain and
      rod;
Who made his brother a chattel, his sister a shameful thing,
   And spat, in his arrogant pride, at the hand of God.

For a blight is over his land, a skeleton sits at his hearth;
   His crown is dragged in the mire, and his throne is a seat of
      shame.
And he in his insolent pride shall perish from off the earth,
   While the coming ages shall blush to hear his name.

SEPTEMBER, 1863.

NON RESPONDAT.

A WIDOW lives across the way,
   Lonely and sad, in sable weeds:
  With her own hands she clothes and feeds
Herself and little daughter, May.

I see her in the early dawn
   Busy about her daily toil,
   Tilling the mellow garden soil
Or dressing weeds from out the lawn.

And later still I see her sit
   With busy needle at her door,
   While fitful shadows on the floor
With every zephyr wave and flit.

The weary gurgling of the rill,
   The honey bee's low monotone,
   The waving shade, the pine trees' moan,
The lowing kine upon the hill,

The robins in their leafy screens,
   All, all remind her of the Lost
   Who calmly sleeps with white hands crossed,
Beneath the sod at New Orleans.

He was but one among the throng
  Who nobly fought at Pleasant Hill,
  And many a gallant fellow will
Be missed as sadly and as long.

But I have lost a brother, and
  The widow mourns by night and day
  The father of her little May
Who molders in his grave of sand.

We grieve; but we are proud to know,
  When plunging shot and shrieking shell
  Made Pleasant Hill an earthly hell,
His face was ever to the foe.

O fearless heart and ready hand!
  O brother of my early youth
  Whose word was synonym for truth,
We greet thee in thy bed of sand.

Thy calm brave face and eye serene
  We may not look upon again;
  But we will keep, thro' joy and pain,
The leaves of memory evergreen.

SIXTY-FIVE AND JOHN BULL.

AH, Sixty-five, you have but brought
 Us the beginning of the end.
We have some grave mistakes to mend,
Some claims to press that may be fraught
 With danger to another shore,
Whose skilled builders drew and planned,
Whose merchant princes built and manned
 Such pirates as the Shenandoah.

You crammed our ears with neutral laws
 Against the stomach of our sense.
 Your statutes were but thin pretense,
And only valued for their flaws.
 You played the Algerine, John Bull.
You laid your cruisers on our track
And furnished clubs to break our back
 Just when you saw our hands were full.

You little thought four years to be
 A lifetime for the stars and bars,
 While yet the war-stained stripes and stars
Should proudly float on every sea.

And so you did a foolish thing :
You turned upon us in our need,
Bartered a nation's faith for greed,
   And kneeled to Cotton as a king.

A staunch, strong friend you might have made
   Of this free nation, but you chose
   Your friends among our deadly foes,
And squared your honor with your trade.
   Thousands of loyal men and true
Sleep underneath the ocean's waves
Or slowly rot in nameless graves
   Who had been living but for you.

You swept our commerce from the seas :
   You have a commerce of your own ;
   And custom, gray with ages grown
Bids us resent such wrongs as these.
   They lie who say we favor strife ;
But we can plant a telling blow
By land or sea, on any foe,
   Who aims against the nation's life.

Be thine, O Sixty-five, the meed
That guerdons valorous thought and deed.
Thou shalt stand out in bold relief
Among the years, the first and chief.

We are too near these huge events
To see their grandeur.   Ages hence,
When time and distance lend a hue
Of mild enchantment to the view,
Let future generations say
For what we battled in our day.

Let struggling nations then decide
If it were selfishness or pride,
Or if the cause which Freedom dowers
Be not their own, as well as ours.

NEW YEAR'S ODE.

WRITE me an ode, the printer said;
　　A sonnet for the new born year
　That cometh with its freight of fear,
And doubt, and hope, and nameless dread.

Alas! is this a time to wield
　In trifling mood an idle pen?
　The world shakes with the tread of men;
A million soldiers are afield.

To-day, the all-time question rings
　In Sinaic tones throughout the land,
　"Shall any self-ruled nations stand?
Or are we born that priests and kings

May rule and ride us?"　And to solve
　The question come the crash of arms,
　And smoking towns, and war's alarms,
And daring deed and high resolve.

The rotten thrones of Europe reel
　As crimson dims the bayonet's glance,
　And ring of saber, ax and lance
Answers the clang of armed heel:

Emperors and kings grow pale with dread
   As from afar they scan the scene,
   Each wishing each to intervene,
Each fearing for his throne and head.

For, underneath each crown and throne
   Upheave a thousand years of wrong.
   The monarch fears a poet's song ;
The people bow their necks and groan ;

But not forever.   They have found
   That thrones can fall and monarchs flee.
   Mine is no gift of prophecy,
Yet as the circling years roll round,

I hear a little bird that sings
   The people by and by shall be
   The stronger : and that time shall see
The last of hierarchs and kings.

Poor Freedom, faint and wan, to-day
   Is up for trial.   And the cause
   Of equal rights and equal laws
Leans heavily on the array

Of armed hosts.   For, since the flood,
   While tyrants ruled and cowards quailed,
   One simple rule has never failed,
Freedom must be baptised in blood!

Such is the rule.   And when the surge
  Of charging columns shakes the plain,
  And rich red blood pours out like rain,
Brave men shall sing no funeral dirge,

But raise a grand old battle shout,
  Such as the Norseman raised of old,
  When, bursting from his mountain hold
He put the southern hosts to rout.

Our bitter trial days will pass
  So surely as the Summer rain
  Will bring song birds and flowers again,
With billowy fields of grain and grass.

And those who, fighting, nobly fell,
  Shall win a nation's all time thanks.
  Where death swept down their serried ranks
They slumber peacefully and well.

Then let us sing no sad refrain.
  The days are glorious, if but we
  With eyes of faith and hope will see
The old prelude, in grander strain,
  Played o'er again to Liberty.

JANUARY 1, 1863.

CRUSADING THE OLD SALOON.

SCENE FIRST.

'TWAS three o'clock of an afternoon,
    And trade was brisk in the old saloon.
Old Schaeffer sat in his office-chair,
With red mustache and well-combed hair,
With pipe, and slippers, and pot of beer,
And face betokening much good cheer;
While Hans and Peter brought ready mugs,
Or rattled the demijohns, barrels and jugs;
And plump Katrina, behind the bar,
Kept track of the money for her papa.
The old dog dozed in a sunny spot,
Or crept in the shade when it grew too hot.
The parrot, a native of hot Para,
Walked, upside down, on his prison bar—
Or, catching the pungent scent of cheese,
Blasphemed in villainous Portuguese;
While three little mice with bellies white,
Kept turning a wheel from morn till night.

And all, on that pleasant Summer day,
Drank friendly beer, and were blithe and gay,
While the sun, with a mellow face of gold,
Looked in, and laughed at the stories told.

SCENE SECOND.—ENTER CRUSADERS.

There came a patter of gaitered feet,
And chattering voices on the street,
And cheeping, peeping noises aloof,
Like a thousand sparrows upon the roof ;
And the pipe fell away from the red mustache
And the beer-mug went by the board with a crash,
And a deadly nightmare horror arose
Till it blanched the color in Schaeffer's nose,
As there entered a tall, snap-eyed old maid
With thirty followers, on a raid,
And Schaeffer groaned, "'Tis der d——d crusade!"
They swarmed like bees at the open door,
Crowded the bar, and covered the floor,
And when they had it their own sweet way,
The snap-eyed woman said, " Let us pray!"
They prayed and chorused their level best,
That over the country, from east to west,
These liquor-sellers—these human ghouls—
Might cease from ruining precious souls;
Till all the people, from sea to sea,
Should sing the praises of Cambric tea,

And men, picked out of the moral mud,

Should sound the glories of Noah's flood,

While all, despising fever or shake,

Should drink spring water, their thirst to slake.

Old Schaeffer listened with open mouth,

The parrot wished himself at the South,

The dog crept under a beer-keg shelf,

And each of the mice took care of himself.

While of drinkers, smokers, bummers and beats,

Nothing was left but the vacant seats.

Slowly and solemnly Schaeffer rose,

The color returned to cheeks and nose.

Sadly he mounted his office-chair,

And scratched for thought in his yellow hair,

Till, partly in anger, partly in grief,

In broken English he found relief :

" Vot der tuyvel dis vomans all do here ?

Vot is it your pizness apout mine beer ?

Ven you got some pizness ov your own,

'Tis petter you leaf mine house alone.

You got some papies ? you got some house ?

You ole fool vomans ! *Das maks nix ous!*

Hans, shump on der stool und open der door,

And let dem dree leedle mouse on der floor ! "

SCENE THIRD.

And Hans, quick turning a button about,

Let three little white-bellied mice jump out,

Suddenly silencing prayer and song
As they scattered and scampered among the throng.
They scratched up stocking-legs, azure and white,
In vain endeavors to climb out of sight.
In columns and volumes of crinoline
They strove to hide where they couldn't be seen.
And that crusade mounted the stools and kegs,
With skirts hugged tightly around their legs.
While the grim, tall leader of their ranks,
With dress well twisted about her shanks,
And short hair bristling upon her scalp,
Stood on a barrel and screamed for help,
Till, seeing a chance for safe retreat,
She led a charge for the open street,
And the crusade rout became complete.

MORAL.

If three little mice can put to flight
An army that battles for " truth and right,"
Is't likely they'll close old Schaeffer's house,
Or stop his lager ? *Nix cum arous.*

TEMPERANCE SONG.

TUNE, " ALL ON HOBBIES."

June, 1874. " The crusade " has reached Wellsboro—in an epidemic form.
There is a wild feminine violence about it—an intensity of weak ferocity, so to
speak, that is prophetic of a brief reign. I tried, by request, to compose a tem-
perance song for the crusaders, but the afflatus petered out on a strong incline
toward whiskey—worse luck

I N coming down Main street I happened to meet
A rosy-checked damsel crusading the street,
And as she was well spoken and pleasant to see,
I allowed her to run a crusade upon me,
 CHORUS.—All on toddy ;
   Good by toddy !
   Oh let everybody
   Go total on tea !

This sweet little damsel was free to maintain
We were losing our labor and wasting our grain
In maintaining a traffic—as bad as could be,
While the number of drunkards was—fearful to see,

CHORUS.—Who all drank toddy ;
        Got drunk on toddy !
        Oh let everybody ·
        Go total on tea !

She ground the old arguments down to an edge,
And ended at length by presenting a pledge,
Which she hinted 'twould be my salvation to sign—
But I modestly told her, not any in mine,
    CHORUS—For I like toddy,
        Hot whiskey toddy ;
        Why should everybody
        Their freedom resign ?

O'LEARY'S LAMENT.

The following little lament may be truthful, if not poetical. It expresses the feelings of my Irish friend, Thomas O'Leary, late of Innisowen.

I WISH I was in Innisowen,
　　In Michael Hennessy's ould shebeen.
'Tis there I'd see bright wathers flowin'
Wid shamrock green an' roses blowin'—
　　For-bye a noggin of ould poteen.

Me heart is sick wid this paradin'
　　Of all the wimmin upon the sthreet,
While they are on the town crusadin'
The fires upon the hearth are fadin',
　　The gossoons cry wid cowld bare feet

Oh let us dhrink—in moderation,
　　To aise our sadness an' banish gloom.
Sure, many a glutton in this nation
While praychin' temp'rance and salvation
　　Has *ate* himself into the tomb.

WELLSBORO AS A TEMPERANCE TOWN.

Under local option regime, Johnny O'Shea suffers from drouth, which the crusade bids fair to make chronic. The following song epitomises his idea of the matter.

OH Wellsboro' isn't at all like a pra'rie,
The hills round about it are lofty an' ah'rary,
The bar-rooms are like the dhry sands of Sahara,—
There's nothing to dhrink whin the Pilgrim is dhry.

There's river an' mountain,
There's streamlet an' fountain ;
There's springs beyond countin'
That niver run dhry.
But whin a man's bate
Wid the drouth an' the hate,
Sure he has no retrate
For a dhrop of ould rye.

This nate little town is the bate of all places
For rosy cheeked girls wid the brightest of faces.
Ye may dance, av ye like, wid the muses an' graces—
But there's nothing to dhrink whin the Pilgrim is dhry.

There's praychers and taychers,

There's lawyers an' docthors;

There's judges an' procthors

   All causes to thry.

But whin a man's bate

Wid the dust an' the hate,

He may walk off his fate

   For a dhrop of ould rye.

'Tis there ye may hear the swate thrush or the linnet,

Aich mornin' at daylight they're sure to begin it,

But divil the dhrop of good whiskey is in it—

There's nothing to dhrink whin the Pilgrim is dhry.

   Then give your bright wathers

   To fishes an' others,

Wid the herons an' cranes that are wadin' the shore.

   Sure, a man is no porpus

   To wather his corpus,

Whin he may have wine an' good whiskey galore.

CPSIA information can be obtained
at www.ICGtesting.com
Printed in the USA
BVOW11s0941120118
504931BV00002B/208/P